CHANGING
SCENES

BENJAMIN WINTERBORN S.J.

CHANGING
SCENES

with a foreword by
CARDINAL BASIL HUME
Archbishop of Westminster

Illustrations by George Adamson

Oxford   New York   Toronto   Melbourne
OXFORD UNIVERSITY PRESS
1980

Oxford University Press, Walton Street, Oxford OX2 6DP

OXFORD LONDON GLASGOW
NEW YORK TORONTO MELBOURNE WELLINGTON
KUALA LUMPUR SINGAPORE JAKARTA HONG KONG TOKYO
DELHI BOMBAY CALCUTTA MADRAS KARACHI
NAIROBI DAR ES SALAAM CAPE TOWN

British Library Cataloguing in Publication Data
Winterborn, Benjamin
  Changing scenes.
  1. Christian life—Catholic authors
  I. Title
  248'.9'2   BX2350.2   79-41029

  ISBN 0-19-213226-1
  ISBN 0-19-213227-X Pbk

Nihil obstat: Rev. E. Yarnold S.J.
Imprimi potest: The Most Rev. George Patrick Dwyer,
Archbishop of Birmingham

*Phototypeset in V.I.P. Palatino by
Western Printing Services Ltd, Bristol
and printed in Great Britain by
Lowe & Brydone Printers Ltd, Thetford, Norfolk*

Contents

Through all the changing scenes of life,
  In trouble and in joy,
The praises of my God shall still
  My heart and tongue employ.

From the hymn by N. Tate and N. Brady

Foreword

I am pleased to write this short Foreword to Father Benjamin Winterborn's book. He and I have known each other for a good many years. I admire the strength of will and determination he has shown in producing this book despite considerable difficulties.

'Changing Scenes' is essentially the result of lived experience—a series of reflections on life, suffering, death, the Church, being 'talked out loud' after a lifetime of pastoral service as a Catholic priest and a Jesuit.

Father Winterborn has written this book for ordinary folk 'in the crowded smoky old village pub' as he puts it. Its anecdotes and reflections are full of distilled wisdom. It is also a revealing book, exposing the author's genuine love of people, his deep interest in them and in their sufferings and problems, and his desire to help them grow in the knowledge and love of God. May his book do just that.

CARDINAL BASIL HUME
Archbishop of Westminster

Preface

MOST Catholic priests who work on a parish find themselves eventually caught up in the lives of their parishioners so that they come to share in many of those hopes and unexpected joys, troubles and sometimes tragic disappointments which make up family life. Not only is the priest, like any other minister of religion, called on to help with baptisms, marriages, and funerals, but, given time, he finds himself treated as if he were a member of the extended family, a sort of honorary uncle, who can always be relied upon to help. Because of the trust which others give him he may easily acquire an inflated sense of his own wisdom, an exaggerated idea of his own personal responsibility; but to be fair to him he certainly wants to help. Naturally enough he will want to create and welcome opportunities to pass on some of those insights which he has found have proved helpful to others in the past; this explains the purpose of this book.

When working on a parish in the early fifties I found most people needed encouragement, but especially converts, and those bereaved, bewildered, or depressed. Today the need is greater. Traditional landmarks hidden or swept away, the very fabric of the only society we are likely to know apparently disintegrating around us—a trite phrase so often heard but nonetheless true—and our vision of the Church as the visible rock of ages modified, and difficult to reconcile with the apparently endless adolescent talk, and calls for action, more reminiscent of student debating societies than the Church we thought we knew. We sense the sub-culture in which we were once so safely wrapped getting leaky at the seams. Sudden changes can create a sense of panic, especially for the old and sick, but not only for them; and most of us find from time to time that we cannot easily summon up the physical and mental energies we need to face new situations. Usually after the crisis, when the dust has settled and the screaming headlines have been forgotten, life is not so very different from the past we used to know, and such adaptations, changes, or confrontations as are really called for are well within our compass. Even so, we may experience a sense of loss. Our Lord insisted 'Fear not', nor should we.

This is an intensely personal book. The reflections are my own about those attitudes to life, God, people and the institutional Catholic Church which I have found helpful. I have sought by anecdote to illustrate what, in a simple way, amounts to a philosophy of life, suffering, death, and the underlying happiness which faith can bring to all men. Part of my point would be that many men live by faith though they don't know it. I would especially wish to encourage those whom Rahner calls the 'anonymous Christians', and those who think their faith is dead. As St. Paul said to the Athenians, 'the God whom I proclaim is in fact the one whom you already worship without knowing it'.

I had thought of calling this the 'the reflections of an anti-mugwump'. As is well known, a mugwump is one who sits on a fence with his mug on one side and his wump on the other until the iron enters his soul. Not a future one would wish for one's friends. To make decisions, even wrong ones, usually leads to greater happiness. This requires courage and trust in ourselves, in our friends, and in God's Holy Spirit, who was promised and has been given. When we reflect we realize we are never quite alone. This should fan our faith.

I hope these reflections will provide grounds to hold firm, to hope, and to fan sparks of faith within us so that we may be encouraged, warmed, and enlivened. Surely we should not expect less from the good news of Christ.

Mr. Denis Kelly, the Recorder of Oxford, Dr. Jonathan Gould, and Peter and Anne Montague gave me much needed initial encouragement when I was wondering if I was wasting my time. My physical energies at that time were very weak and it was difficult to tell whether the thoughts in my mind could be put successfully into book form. Then, once I had been encouraged, an American Jesuit, Father Caspar Miller, who has been working in Nepal for the last twenty years, and Father Jack Quinn S.J. from the University of Scranton, Pennsylvania, showed such enthusiasm that I had to keep writing.

In preparing the book for press, I owe a debt of deep gratitude to Father Edward Yarnold, to the staff of the Oxford University Press, and to Mrs. Dorothy Heapy, who sub-edited the manuscript and made many positive suggestions. Such faults as remain are my own, and but for the help of my good friends they would have been legion.

Finally I would want to thank countless nurses in the Radcliffe Infirmary, the Acland Nursing Home, SS John and Elizabeth Hospital in London, and many people who enabled me so to convalesce that I could manage to write while doing so. I can only hope that I did not try their patience too hard—as people with 'messages' so often do—and that the reader may experience some of the joy and happiness I found when writing it.

B. W.

January 1979

1   The world in the pub

WHEN I was a child, I knew a country village through which ran a tiny stream. The experts long ago had decided that this small sluggish stretch of water should mark the boundary between Sussex and Kent. Centuries later, in our own day, the Catholic authorities decided that the diocese of Arundel and Brighton should be formed with boundaries coterminous with those of the county of Sussex. The result, which no one wished, was that this country village was split between two dioceses, with the nearest Catholic church four miles away to east or west according to one's preference. The village was now officially defined as something it had always been, a spiritual no-man's-land, difficult to find like so many of those places where one wants to go, lying as it did on the crack or fold of the map. It was easily neglected, and has become to my slightly frenzied mind a symbol and a type of what many a good man finds his own state to be in the world today.

In such a place, and for such a man, all the talk of the role of the laity in the Church, the building up of growth points for the future, identifying with the poor and changing the social order so as to bring justice to the Third World, the talk of relevance and racialism, even the talk of community, seemed to belong to a different world.

It was not that the villagers or those whom I think they typify were unwilling or unconcerned, but they lived their own lives in a world of their own and, for the most part, being farmers, had no time for television. They had always been a village community; the railway had passed them by, and the country bus only visited them at infrequent intervals, as one could see from the timetable in the village Post Office. They did not complain. Why should they? They had their own lives to lead, and their children were well cared for in a neighbouring school. The village shops catered for most of their needs.

Sometimes the talk about ecumenism seemed to them to strike a false note. Even the oldest in the village could not remember the day when the parson and the priest had not been on friendly terms, though the one was a pillar of the place, and the other only an occasional though friendly visitor. They had their get-togethers, bazaars, fêtes and fairs, but spiritually the place seemed more dead than alive—though who were we to judge?—

> The smoky crowded village pub was like
>   Parliament for them,
> For all were represented
> And all could have their say,
> And there were always helping hands
> For anyone in need;
> The sick and widowed were not there,
> Nor were the motherless tots,
> But in a gathering like that
> Their needs were not forgot.

Alas, I never knew such a pub, but the village pub epitomizes something of the good-natured earthy spirit which you can find in so many corners of the world. The atmosphere may not be exactly spiritual, certainly not pious, but underneath the horsey talk and the crude jokes which accompany the pint of ale and the more sophisticated 'gin and it' you always seem to find the same basic goodness and concern to help those in need. It was and is impossible to imagine such people as very far from the Kingdom of God. They would for the most part have called themselves Christians and would certainly have been prepared to die to save others, as so many have shown themselves ready to do in recent years; yet such men and women give only a passing nod towards the institutional Churches.

Sometimes I wonder if the Establishment has not done almost incalculable harm to the cause of Christianity in England. It has made Christianity respectable. Not that I would wish to make it disreputable, but no priest or minister of religion would want to sail under false colours. One wants to be considered respectable only on the basis of what one says and does and is, and not just because one wears the right tie, or dog-collar, or turtle-necked sweater as the case may be. We live in a society where everything is labelled, and people like to label the Churches and their ministers as a 'Good Thing'. Certainly I would agree. But once we ministers as individuals accept the label, we find we lose our freedom, and are expected to conform to a pattern; to be what others expect us to be, to behave as society thinks we should behave. No longer can we easily fit unnoticed into that smoky crowded room in the old village pub. We don't belong. Whether we like it or not, the clergy are men apart, and if society as a whole respects them, respected they will be, and they will have to walk within the confines of that category, or opt out and join the ranks of the clergy anonymous.

That could be said with equal truth of the respectability of generals, or admirals, or judges, of barristers, politicians, policemen, bankers or business men, or even of. . . . I sometimes wonder where one should put that little hesitating note. Somewhere along the line a doubt occurs and one hesitates as to whether this or that profession is still quite as respectable as it used to be.

But the Establishment has given the Church of England

clergy an extra-special coating of respectability and, in our own lifetime, possibly because of the example of the chaplains in the services during the two World Wars and the way they courageously identified themselves with the needs of their country and their men, this extra coating of respectability now covers Catholic priests and all the other ministers of the other denominations as well.

The difficulty about Establishment and respectability, as I see it, is that they have nothing to do with Christianity, and indeed easily become stumbling-blocks rather than helps in the work which the Churches are trying to do, in that they distract people from the main work. So long as that decent chap in the pub feels he can get by with an occasional nod in the direction of Christ, and with a kindly word of encouragement to the vicar going on his various rounds of mercy, why should he bother to do more? If asked, he will contribute generously to the poor of the parish, and will even give his time and expertise to sort out the parish accounts and the finances and administration of the school and club. He's a very decent fellow, and welcomes the vicar or parish priest occasionally—not too often—to his pub or to his home. It's all highly respectable, typically Anglo-Saxon and practical. He wants to keep a level head. He does not want to catch religion. And who can blame him? Who would? The example of some who have caught religion in the past has not unreasonably frightened away many a good man who has ducked, taken cover, or run for his life. He has valued his sanity too much.

It seems so difficult to get things right. In the old days we used to say that 'grace builds on nature'; that just as the sad saint is a sad sort of a saint, so too the eccentric and fanatic are both unbalanced and underdeveloped in that they only see things from what is usually rather a narrow point of view. They may see things very clearly and sometimes have some insight and such penetration as to make them feel very strongly, but, to change the metaphor, they need fattening up on the whole truth and not merely on one aspect of that truth, however important it may be. They need to be rounded off.

The Old Testament prophets must have been uncomfortable people to live with, and, though their insights were clearly always relevant and of great immediate significance, when they delivered their messages the sparks were apt to fly. It is not too difficult for us, with hindsight, to see that this was clearly what God wanted, so that his chosen people could become properly earthed and rooted in the truth.

As we look back with our own limited knowledge over the history of time we can, I think, justly reflect that there has probably never been a day, nor ever will there be, when something similar will not be needed to rouse us out of our apathy and self-complacency. To remain a mere onlooker presupposes a comfortable sort of philosophy of life when you can identify easily with everyone in the village pub, and be known as a decent fellow. But is that good enough, and in the long run is it even possible? Are we living in a fool's paradise? We are all living on the heritage of the past; whilst the values we know and in which we believe are everywhere disintegrating around us, we innocently assume that life can still go on unchanged; that men will always try to be the sort of decent chaps, perhaps a bit goofy with a twisted logic all their own, whom we used to know, good pagans; that justice and concern for those in need, unselfishness, loyalty, honesty and decency are part of the very make-up of mankind; that heaven is a continuation of the happy home we used to know as children; that the future is inevitably a continuation of the past; that all will yet be well if we sit tight. But what if my home was not so happy, what if our present is a state of being lonely and forlorn, what have we then to look forward to?

If we look at the world around us a little more realistically we see everywhere the breakdown of family life, the increases in abortions, and violence towards the old and young and sick; the rejection of honesty in almost every walk of life. Child pornography and some of the inhumanity of man to man seem to have reached depths and proportions unknown to previous times. We only have to read the papers to know that all is far from well in the world today.

I remember a young couple who were appalled by the dis-
crimination against the blacks in the USA in the early sixties.
They need not have done anything. They were English, and it
was not a problem of their own making. But as Christians they
felt they could not live in peace surrounded by injustice. They
could not hope to put the world to rights overnight, but they
could and did use their heads and hearts to try to help a desperate situation. Later they went to Africa, and once again managed
both to keep their heads and also to speak out for those who had
no one to fight their cause. Subsequently they did something
similar to help those living in the slums in England. They were
large-hearted, and gave hope wherever they went.

I think the crowded smoky old village pub includes many
such men and women who are decent people, but who, alas,
take their faith for granted, and see it as just a gift of God for
themselves and not for all mankind. But the Good News is for
all the world, for people as they are. The crowds who gather in
the pubs may not seem to be, and probably never will be, the
hub of the universe, or the matrix which will alter the destinies
of man. They may indeed be just a village community, a
spiritual no-man's-land, not a growth point for the future, and
of very limited value in the eyes of the V.I.P.s of this world.
Was Bethlehem any greater in its day?

It is for men and women like those, and not for the clever
kind, that I want to write these words. Their faith is often
dormant, and adds but little savour to their lives. The flickering lamps in their hearts need only a tiny twist to be turned on
full, and then their light would shine all through the land.
They are so full of a natural reserve, so anxious not to impose
their own personal views on others, so conscious of their own
inadequacy to express the faith in their hearts, that they dare
not even encourage themselves. It is their natural virtues
which seem to hinder their faith from flowering in their lives.
What do they need? How can they be helped? They are not a
no-man's-land, but represent that all-important place where
the focus of faith and the world are for ever locked in battle: the
heart of man.

2   Facing life

OUR memories are like well-stocked libraries, full of those favourite books and records which belong to us alone. Only we possess a key, but we are free to dip into those treasures as we will. When problems arise, in some new difficult situation, there is nearly always a memory from our past we can recall to give us help. As time goes by the library grows richer. There is much to be said for old age.

Many of our memories will be of people, unique and unforgettable, but sometimes they will be of scenes we cannot quite recapture or ever quite forget. I find that seascapes are amongst the most elusive of childhood memories. The sea was every day so different, it had so many moods, now angry, now enticing, sometimes almost sullen, often playful. The cloud formations scudding across the huge expanse of sky provided an ever-changing backcloth for the varied moods of the sea.

We would crunch, rather than walk, across the shingle, always expecting to find a hidden treasure. We could walk the same stretch day by day, with unabated hopes and expecta-

tions which were never sated, and make our way across the
tangled seaweed towards the firmer sand where the high tide
and the shingle used to meet. In a world where almost everything was shifting, the long concrete retaining wall built to
keep the spring tides from encroaching on the road beyond
stood out unchanged. We used to throw stones in the sea, and
wonder how you could get bored if you lived beside it and
could watch the breaking of the waves and listen to the roar.
Exhausted by the beauty of the scene, which seemed like
heaven, too vast for us to grasp or understand, we turned,
almost in desperation, to collect the tiny lovely shells which
always filled us with a new delight.

Meanwhile the greedy gulls overhead were piercing the air
with their shrill cries as they whirled and pounced and fought
for scraps of food.

We threaded our way between the fishing-boats drawn up
along the shore, tripping over the ropes half-buried in the
sand, and quickly came to the tall wooden fishermen's huts
which looked so black and small against the white of the
massive chalk cliffs behind. The strong smell of tar from the
huts and boats and the flotsam and jetsam and pieces of old
cork and wreckage gave the salty air a pungency which has
survived through all the years. Ahead, the cliffs dominating
the old harbour town came down to meet the sea, and we
could walk no further.

On that last final dirty stretch of shingle sand and jagged
rocks beneath the cliffs, the fishermen's nets were stretched
out taut across long poles and lay drying in the sun. Their
squared meshes, like giant crosswords, had been pulled this
way and that into a variety of different shapes. I often used to
think this was not a bad image of life itself. So many hidden
factors contribute to make us what we are, and we in turn
affect the lives of others. A break within the net, or a large
catch, and all the meshes are placed under an added strain.
Instead of squares they take on the shapes of diamonds with
sharp pointed corners, and the pattern of the whole is
changed. So with our lives.

When we are young we think that life lies at our feet and is there for the taking; that we are free to fashion it at will. Slowly we learn this is not true. We all depend in many secret hidden ways upon each other, yet, even so, there is much more that we, alone, can do.

Recently I got a letter from a small girl of seven. 'I am so bored,' she complained, 'life has so little to offer.' The summer holidays had been too long. What, I wondered, did she expect from life? It is a problem which recurs, but more difficult to answer than it used to be, especially for those just leaving school.

In the physical world around us most things grow in fits and starts. There are periods of sudden growth, when, we are told, those with ears more sensitive than most can hear the rhubarb, or is it the cabbages, growing in the stillness of the night. We expect visible growth in the spring and decay in the depths of the winter, yet for some curious reason we expect to grow steadily ourselves.

I often recall a class of twelve-year-olds in which two boys were quite outstanding, head and shoulders above the rest. On the rugby field they could push their way easily through the mob of smaller boys. One of the two, the tallest, never grew again, and even before he left school he was dwarfed by his contemporaries and ended up in middle age a smaller man than most. Differences of physical growth amongst the young may disappoint us, but do not cause us much surprise. Yet we do tend to become upset when we experience in ourselves unpredictable periods of apparent intellectual and spiritual stagnation after times of sudden growth in what we like to think of as our creative selves. Periods of exciting personal growth, when a child, for instance, having just learnt to read, will avidly devour all knowledge that comes his way, are often re-enacted in later life. A good teacher, a perceptive girl or boy-friend, or parents, children or grandchildren may provide the necessary stimulation. Sometimes the motivation which causes unexpected growth in later life may be due to the challenge of a new job, the opportunities for a new experience, or the acceptance of a new responsibility. Normally, though, we have to wait upon events; the stimulus comes to us from outside ourselves.

We are not unlike the sea, with all its different moods, influenced by and influencing too the sky and all with which it comes in contact; every day so different, yet every day the same. So too with us: our inner identity remains apparently unchanged, not unlike the shingle, for ever shifting under the roaring breaking of the waves. When we are young it is our own personal identity which we value above all else and which we seek to express and to have recognized by others; to which we know we must be true.

It is said of Canning that when he was making his first speech in Parliament he sensed that everyone was against him and making fun of him, and he started to dry up. His friends realized what was happening, and interrupted with uproarious applause. This gave him the encouragement he badly needed, and he went on to make a brilliant speech. With the understanding and support of his friends he succeeded in bringing out the qualities which he knew he had, but could not by himself express. As a result he found himself, and never faltered again.

For many of us, in different ways, we know this is desirable but difficult to attain. Sometimes it may indeed be quite impossible, because we have over-idealistic and unrealistic views of what life is all about. We can so easily think of our life as an inner force within us, for ever growing stronger upwards and outwards and in all directions, so that wisdom and success will most certainly be ours with the passing of the years. Yet we know this is not true. We are, I suspect, unduly influenced by generalized views of evolution which we apply in too facile a way to growth within ourselves, and this augments our expectations of a fullness of life always increasing and depending upon ourselves alone.

The endless interaction of the elemental forces of nature on the sea-shore may give us a truer insight into our own life. We have this inner urge which 'will flame out, like shining from shook foil', even if, as Hopkins said, it has been 'seared with trade; bleared, smeared with toil'. Like beaten gold, or like the massive unhewn stone in which a Michelangelo has seen his masterpiece, we have to be shaped, fashioned, formed, and pulled this way and that so that, like the meshes in the fishermen's net, we may be able to co-operate in something bigger than ourselves, maybe for a catch of fish, or, to change the metaphor, maybe to reflect the grandeur of God in whose likeness we are made.

Once we grasp this fundamental truth, that we are personally involved in the interactions of forces greater than ourselves, then timing becomes all-important. The truths pronounced so many years ago by the writer of *Ecclesiastes* have not lost their significance over the centuries:

> There is a season for everything, a time for every occupation under heaven:
>> A time for giving birth,
>> a time for dying;
>> a time for planting,
>> a time for uprooting what has been planted.
>> A time for killing,
>> a time for healing;
>> a time for knocking down,
>> a time for building.
>> A time for tears,
>> a time for laughter;
>> a time for mourning,
>> a time for dancing.
>> A time for throwing stones away,
>> a time for gathering them up;
>> a time for embracing,
>> a time to refrain from embracing.
>> A time for searching,
>> a time for losing;
>> a time for keeping,
>> a time for throwing away.
>> A time for tearing,
>> a time for sewing;

> a time for keeping silent,
> a time for speaking.
> A time for loving,
> a time for hating;
> a time for war,
> a time for peace.

If we can grasp this fundamental truth we can spare ourselves much frustration and disappointment.

We know that timing makes all the difference in golf, or cricket, or tennis, that the orator, the raconteur, and actor must have a sense of timing; that parents as well as children and all good friends must know when to speak and when to be silent. So too with our decisions and our understanding of the various moods and movements of our lives: the timing must be right.

I remember a priest friend of mine discussing a new project with his superiors. 'We shall have to assess it in two years' time,' they said, 'to see if it has worked.' My good friend became quite indignant, and considered the time allowed him far too short. As he explained, his proposition had to be sold, like any new idea, to suitable men who would, he hoped, develop it. This would take time. In its final form his idea would, he believed, take on a shape and colour which no one in the initial stages could have foreseen. If indeed those who were to run it tried to make it conform to their own past experiences in other fields, or if they sought to label it with their own preconceived images, they would kill the project at birth. So he tried to expound the truth that there is a time for ploughing, a time for sowing and a time for reaping. This same truth applies within our own individual lives.

Yet when we are engaged on what seems like endless preparation and ploughing for the good of future generations, we need encouragement. Limited and intermediate objectives by which we can measure some success are useful. The final fruit may not appear until after we are dead. But we must be realistic in our appraisals about what we are trying to do, and, if we are indeed engaged on the job of ploughing and preparing the ground and trying to plant the seed, we shall only discourage ourselves if we expect instant results to which we can point as signs of success. As any gardener knows, if in such conditions there are signs of sudden growth they are almost certainly weeds, which should not be there and will only hinder our tender plants when they do eventually appear.

I say all this because I think all of us, and the young in particular, need to be encouraged to realize that anything really worthwhile doing will take years to accomplish, and it is given to few men to do that. Most of us are called to co-operate with others in works which no man could do single-handed. This is obviously true within the family, where we all need each other, but equally true within our private individual lives. The callings which stimulate our growth can come in different ways, and when the chance comes we must seize it.

You may have seen a statue of St. Ignatius with a ball at his feet. An unlikely composition, as he was not a man to waste opportunities, and if the ball had been at his feet he would have shot at goal or passed it to another. He was a strong believer in corporate endeavour. But the ball was meant to be the cannon-ball which broke his leg and destroyed the career on which he had set his heart. He had to start again. The ball, a symbol of God's intervention, destroyed his early hopes, his first career, but opened up a vision far greater of something which he could not do alone.

We can so easily restrict our vision to what is immediately possible or desirable, and as a result, without realizing it, we can set our sights too low. We have to try to be ourselves, and yet for the most part we cannot hope to do that except in and through co-operating with, and sometimes rejecting, others. The more we think of life as a steady process the more likely we are to forget that there are sometimes vitally important moments, what the theologians call 'moments of grace', when we must seize the opportunity and take time by the forelock, or the opportunity will be lost for ever. It is as though there was a conjunction of the stars when all things come together—when perhaps our physical, mental and spiritual powers are all at their peak—and when under the grace of God we see our vision clearly and the road opens up before us. At such times we do not need to ask advice, indeed to ask advice may be to court disaster. We need to pray that we are not deceiving ourselves, that it is a worthwhile good we are hoping to achieve. It may be useful to ask myself if, when I come to die and I look back on my life, I shall be glad I seized this opportunity. Indeed shall I be able to live with myself if, having seen this chance, I let it pass? Unless I act without delay the vision can grow dim and becomes a faint memory, haunting me with what might have been. That is a sadness known to most of us. Please God there will be new opportunities, new moments of grace, new visions, but the ones I failed to seize are I think lost for ever—at least in their pristine glory. The timing is all-important.

I have known many young men who have postponed decisions and lived to regret it. They considered the priesthood and did nothing about it. They thought that as long as they continued to think idly about it the opportunity to pursue a vocation would remain open to them. They were mistaken. I remember talking to one such man who, he thought, had been considering the priesthood for many years. He said, 'I'm still thinking about it.' 'No,' I replied, in my youthful brashness, 'you have already made up your mind; you have decided that you will just continue to think about it, and that is all you will ever do.' Alas, experience showed that I was right. Mere thinking can be an excuse for avoiding decisions. Perhaps he never had a vocation, perhaps it may turn out to be a late vocation and in his sixties he may yet receive the grace to follow a call which has haunted him since his early teens. I do not know. But sometimes I am sure we deceive ourselves by thinking that by thinking we can absolve ourselves from action.

I well remember one young man who had a particular girlfriend for over five years and then, when the girl was twenty-six or twenty-seven, he decided to call it off and marry another. He never realized that he had probably ruined the first girl's chances of ever finding a suitable partner. He had monopolized her affections for years when she was young and attractive, and could have had many other suitors, and then, quite suddenly, he had left her in the lurch. It is easy to say it was better to break off the relationship before further damage was done; that had they married both their lives might have been ruined. But somewhere during those years it seemed to me that charity and justice had quite unwittingly been infringed. Perhaps it was partly my fault; I never preached about that subject.

Subsequently I did talk about it in public, and one young man who had been going steady for many years suddenly realized that he was being unfair to his girl; he promptly proposed, and was accepted. He married her and they have, I am glad to say, been married happily ever since.

Sometimes the older generation are blamed unfairly for failing to stress those elementary truths not yet clearly seen by a younger generation. One girl I know wanted to marry a most unsuitable young man. He was her first love, and she was infatuated. Her mother, with whom she got on very well, tried in a roundabout way to point out the glaring unsuitability of the match and, failing in that, she did at least succeed in counselling a reasonable delay before the marriage took place. Before the actual time for the marriage arrived the girl suddenly realized her mistake, and broke off the engagement. She then quite unreasonably complained to her mother, 'Why didn't you point out to me how unsuitable he was, surely you must have seen it.' Had the poor mother done so in so many words, she would almost certainly have driven her daughter into the arms of her erstwhile lover. By her patience she had saved the situation, but she got no thanks.

When I was a young man I wondered if I should become a priest, and asked advice. Fortunately I asked a wise old man who gave me advice which I think was amongst the best I ever received. What he said was: you must make up your own mind. If we accept the fact that God became Man and lived and died because he loved us—incomprehensible and at first sight absurd as such a notion is—then we are faced with the question as to what we ought to do in return. For it has always seemed to me axiomatic that some response is called for if one is to behave honourably.

When St. Thomas More was a young man he thought he should become a priest. He tried his vocation, and decided that the life was not for him, although he always remained attracted by the thought. It was not because he was ungenerous. After all, he was prepared not only to lay down his life but, perhaps even more difficult, he was ready to stand almost alone when good bishops and priests and laymen and apparently admirable people all around him thought he was a fool, and when it meant goodbye—was it, he sometimes must have wondered, an unnecessary goodbye—to his daughter Margaret whom he loved as the darling of his life. He did not lack courage or generosity, but he did not become a priest or even a religious. After much prayer he had decided it was not the life for him.

For myself I cannot begin to understand his motives, but why should I expect to, for however much we seek to articulate our motives and explain them to others, there are always hidden motives, unknown and unsuspected, pulling at our hearts and in our heads, which under the inspiration of the Holy Spirit make up what we call a vocation. We cannot reduce the calling of the Spirit to any form of words. He works in a different dimension, and all we can do is to try to be open to his movements in our hearts and discern—if we are lucky, perhaps with the help of a spiritual director—whether indeed we are listening to the promptings of the Holy Spirit or to the secret murmurings of our own suppressed feelings. The two, of course, may be pulling in harmony, but only one experienced in the things of the Spirit can be a useful guide on such occasions.

But this does not alter the presupposition that one would expect to find most boys and girls thinking about the priesthood and/or religious life sometime in their early life, when all the options are open.

Dear St. Benedict-Joseph Labre, of whom Margaret Monro wrote so beautifully, spent all his life trying to find the 'right' niche in the right religious order. He never found it, and, having lived his life always seeking to find the will of God for him, he died like a common beggar. To live in a fog all one's life, never to see the road opening up before one, means to be called to a life of faith. St. Benedict-Joseph Labre never had any job satisfaction, but he kept on trying, 'searching'. We can see, though he himself could never see it, the unique vocation to which he had been called. He lived all his life hoping to find that blueprint, that role, which would draw him closer to the God he loved. He died apparently a ne'er-do-weel, an utter failure, he did not achieve anything; but those who knew him well realized when he died that he had certainly achieved the highest sanctity, and he was quite rightly acclaimed after his death as a saint of God.

I mention St. Benedict-Joseph Labre because today his example is extremely relevant. Today it is almost impossible for most young men and women when they leave school to know what they should do with their lives. They are lucky if they do feel called to a special vocation, whether it be the priesthood, or the religious life as a brother or sister, or as a member of one of the recognized professions—a doctor, or a vet, a teacher, a nurse, or a social worker. But the vast majority of young people feel no such clear attraction. They may have their 'O' levels, perhaps their 'A' levels, maybe even a degree, and sometimes specific training as a secretary as well, but still the field is too wide open; they can easily become distraught and discouraged, and indeed suffer breakdowns, because they find themselves unwanted and unneeded by the society around them.

I have only a few words of sympathy and advice for the increasing numbers who find themselves in this unenviable plight. In the first place they must seek to avoid becoming discouraged, or all is lost. There are no blueprints, no easy solutions, and they must be content to face the fact that perhaps for several years they will have to live with an uncertain future about them. The older generation, who knew security and were accustomed to a settled way of life, have not been helpful in this matter. I knew old men who, having lived their lives in the Indian army, were appalled when they heard of young men of twenty-two, twenty-eight, or even thirty-five changing their jobs, even though they were married and had children to care for. To the red-faced fiery old colonel twisting his moustache such behaviour was irresponsible. He was no longer in touch with the realities of life. But habits die slowly, and even today many a youngster will find that people expect him to sort out his career before he leaves school, or at least by the time he leaves the university; whereas in practice, with the best will in the world, he may not find this possible. The increased number of the unemployed amongst school-leavers is no reflection on the young, but a terrible indictment on the older generation. Today it has become a fact of life that it is increasingly difficult for the young to find a suitable slot where they can hope to be reasonably happy.

The first and most important thing is for them to face the reality as it is, and to refuse to become depressed. They may have to go on trying for months and even years before they can get the job they want. They must not read into this delay a sign of their inadequacy, but see it as a fault in society, not themselves.

In the second place, they must not expect to find even a suitable job in the first instance. They are usually best advised to start with any job, however humble. They need experience, and only a job will give them some of that. They may not like the job, and may quickly learn that even though they don't know exactly what they want, at least they know some of the things they want to avoid.

Thirdly, they must have courage, courage to take up a job they never really wanted, and courage to give it up if it does not work out as they would have wished; courage to admit mistakes; courage and resilience to go on trying; courage, even late in life, to be prepared to face new challenges and even more drudgery of further training; courage, if married, to be open with their partners about their hopes and failures, their fears and aspirations. Courage, too, sometimes not to be open with their children, as the young need all the security they can get, and should not be needlessly exposed to the traumas of decision-making which are necessary for their parents. Courage to accept the fact that a second career is rapidly becoming a norm of life; even a third career which will accompany or precede retirement is already seen as desirable. Where should we put the limits? I speak with some experience as one who, as a priest, has had many different assignments, and found them all worth while.

Sometimes a man takes on a job, and then finds he has married a situation which demands not just his time but all his energies, mental and emotional, sleeping and waking. He has to ask himself: is this how he can best spend his short time on earth, and if so for how long? and is it fair to his wife and to his children? Today the problem seems to be increasing, jobs are more demanding, so no wonder more and more young people seek an alternative society and opt out of the rat-race. They want to live their own lives if only they can find the ways and means. They don't always want a car or a television, or even a fridge, but they must find the wherewithal to exist in a society which tends to encroach and control more and more of our domestic lives. Such people need to keep unsullied the courage of their convictions. In their own way they will always be, like the monks of old and the spires of the country parish churches, a witness to values which surpass this materialistic world in which we live. That may well be their true vocation.

If the object of the artist is to shake people out of their preconceived ideas of beauty, and to shock or entice them to see something of the beauty and grandeur of the world which is always about them, and which so easily escapes attention; and if it is the function of the stars as they pursue their heavenly courses to repel and attract millions of other stars, so that, as they all interact, each and every one of them fulfills a purpose only discernible many light-years away, who can put a limit to the influence which one small individual may have on those with whom he comes in contact? That surely is his vocation here and now, whatever may lie in the future.

I suspect we have all known many men and women, and children too, who have been mentally or physically handicapped from birth. 'What a tragedy', so many people say. But those of us who have been privileged to know families where one of the members was handicapped in some way have always found that, once the situation has been accepted, once love has been allowed to dominate the initial disappointment, then a new dimension of happiness has entered the whole family. In a most extraordinary way the family usually seems able to benefit from what looked like a disaster. Basic values of life have had to be readjusted, and the nonsense so often transmitted by the media has had to be unmasked by the realities of life. Although the handicapped child or aged relative impedes mobility, and may even prevent family holidays away from home, yet the handicapped add a quality and dimension and happiness of greater value than anything which money could have achieved.

Worthwhile opportunities do not always look attractive at first sight, and it requires faith to look below the surface. In his *Confessions* St. Augustine wrote:

> All ask what they wish
> but do not always hear the answer they wish.
> That man is your best servant
> who is not so much concerned to hear from you
>   what he wills,
> As to will what he hears from you.

3   One-parent families

I

AMONGST the most tragic figures of today are the young women, and sometimes the young men, who have been left alone to face life with their children, but without their married partner. On many occasions I have wondered what one can or should write to such people. Here are some of my reflections which I hope may be helpful.

It was raining. The room was cold, drab. The steady roar of traffic provided the illusion that I was not alone. However hard I stared the thoughts refused to flow. I knew I had to write, but what could I say? Perhaps by putting my reflections down on paper I could stimulate the grey cells.

I had known the girl, as I had known many others in similar situations, for many years. They called her Dorothea, I called her 'Dee'. She had four children. Vivacious, friendly, attractive, even beautiful to my unsophisticated eye, she had always been the centre of love and affection in her younger days.

Deservedly so. Even her school reports had praised her qualities of leadership, loyalty, and a certain toughness. They had
been more reserved about her academic qualifications, though
these were adequate, and she had migrated successfully to a
university. Perhaps a butterfly mind—but warm and generous. Made for love. Her husband had not thought so.

The story of the young wife suddenly alone in the world
with her young is infinitely depressing, and every day more
common. Human tragedies usually are. But what could I, a
priest who had known her for so many years, say or do to
comfort her? It was not a new problem. I had tried unsuccess-
fully to face it many times before.

I knew I must do something. I remembered the tragic death
of a friend of mine some years before. I really meant to write to
the parents. I put it off. What could I say? No letter was
written, and the opportunity passed. Too late I knew I had
failed my friend and his parents, beside themselves with grief.
Whatever I could have written would have been inadequate,
but better that than no communication. Fear of failure is a bad
counsellor. Because success as I see it may not be possible,
because from one point of view there cannot be any chance of
success, it does not follow that there may not be much which
can still be done to help. If you cannot save the ship you may
still be able to rescue the crew, and maybe even salvage some
of the cargo too. If you cannot restore a torn limb, you can try
to revive a drooping spirit and help happiness to creep in,
maybe stealthily and unseen.

Death is surely an ultimate. So, too, for a Catholic, is
divorce. To fail to write because one is not God and cannot
wave a magic wand and wipe out the past is surely inexcus-
able. But what to write, and how to encourage and comfort?

'The Lord is my Shepherd . . .' the old words come back.
There are many texts which comforted us in happier times, but
would they help? Were they the answer here and now, or
would one be using them like magic? The inspired Word of
God needs to be handled with care. We should not too easily
assume we have the wisdom of the Holy Spirit for others; in

the first place he is always given to each of us for ourselves. We have to be cautious in giving advice. Looking back on a reasonably long life I can reflect that I have nearly always been wrong when I have asked advice and blindly followed it. Only on two or three occasions can I remember receiving really good advice, and then it was always the same: try to be honest with yourself, weigh the facts, and make up your own mind after you have put them before the Lord.

The girl had lost her other half, her joy for the present, her hope for the future. Her children had lost too—would it be fair to say they had lost more, or less? One cannot judge or equate one sorrow with another any more than one can compare love.

Little girls with long pigtails to their waists crowding round the visiting priest in the school playground long to introduce him to their friends in their special order of preference: 'She is my best friend, she is my second—no, I think my third friend', and so on. All deadly serious, and the order changes from day to day. Lucky to have their love-lives so well ordered.

As one grows older, 'friend' and 'acquaintance', 'love' and 'like'—the nuances multiply. Like St. Thomas's Angels, each loved one becomes unique. Each is so special in his or her own way that comparisons are meaningless. The reverse side of the coin seems equally true; it is meaningless to compare one loss with another.

II

As a Catholic, Dee could not remarry. Was she then destined to lead the rest of her life alone? She was still too young—not more than twenty-eight. Should I encourage her, like a young nun, to look beyond the present and put her faith in God? But a young nun does not just look beyond the present. She is taught to find God in the here and now. As Hopkins wrote:

> The world is charged with the grandeur of God.
> It will flame out, like shining from shook foil;
> It gathers to a greatness, like the ooze of oil
> Crushed. Why do men then now not reck his rod?

No wasted time for the young nun. What then of Dee, the girl to whom I was writing? Surely she too should seek and find God in the here and now, and above all in her children's faces; as Hopkins says, the 'just man'—and surely still more the child—

> Acts in God's eye what in God's eye he is—
> Christ. For Christ plays in ten thousand places,
> Lovely in limbs, and lovely in eyes not his
> To the Father through the features of men's faces.

Perhaps there was salvation and sanity there. Would it be reasonable for me to urge Dee to find herself in her children? She loved them—doted might be a better word for her affection for her youngest—but there was still enough of the young university graduate in her to suggest that she was capable of Higher Things. What do we mean? Higher or Lower, what is the norm?

Financially she was not likely to find a future in her children, though if she were lucky they might indeed look after her in her old age. Seeing them playing on the floor one could more readily imagine they would be a financial liability for many a long day to come. Emotionally mothers know the answers to the unspoken fears and questions of their children, but whether it is more than a sterile academic exercise to try to separate the emotional and rational within this relationship, and to build upon the academic, is doubtful. Some academic exercises seem to be curiously pointless and, apart from keeping those who engage in them reasonably happy and preventing them from doing harm elsewhere, are of no apparent help to mankind. From time to time, like children, we all need to play with bricks so that we can keep our priorities right, take off our masks, be ourselves and not a figment of our imagination. But from time to time we also need to be stretched—and Dee, I think, will have to stretch herself.

If many a don finds that his research profits from the unexpected insights and stimulus which he gets from tutoring a more than usually perceptive student, should not a young mother find not only her own emotional life, but even her own rational, objective academic life also stimulated by her young? Does the 'humani nil a me alienum puto' of Terence stretch down even to the nappy stage? This idea might well be difficult to grasp for a young mother, at a time when her life is so full of physical weariness, monotony, and depression.

Many more fortunate young mothers, who have the support of their husbands behind them, find they cannot afford the time and energy to pursue their academic leanings. Nor yet can Dee. So many young people desperately want to be true to themselves, to find themselves, to fulfil themselves, and hope to do this by pursuing further research or their own particular literary or artistic bent. The results are often tragic. Unless we fulfil our present responsibilities we shall never find ourselves. Too often the pursuit of further studies entails the neglect of far more vital personal relationships with husbands and wives and children.

If Dee is to pursue her longings for intellectual fulfilment she must find a way of fulfilling them within the ambit of her home, and in such a way that her children with their endless questionings will stimulate and not distract her from the work she wants to do.

They say we all learn by experience, and so one should not expect a simple celibate to know the answer. But the logic fits the facts as I have heard and seen them in the lives of others: we find ourselves by fulfilling our immediate responsibilities. This principle, I think, is universal, and applies just as much to priests and religious as it does to young mothers; but it is difficult, and needs great faith to learn.

Apart from physical, mental, spiritual, and emotional growth, there is in every human relationship a dynamic of its own which never ceases to amaze. I have always assumed that it is because I was brought up from an early age to believe that man was made to the image and likeness of God, and because I believe in the Trinity and the dynamic of the inter-relationships of the three Divine Persons, that I have never been surprised to find something analogous and mysterious

in the dynamism which influences all human relationships.

We meet a friend we have not met for years. Impossible to
take up the relationship exactly where it was laid down.
Changes unseen, un-noticed, have taken place. We have been
travelling along the same or parallel roads during the interven-
ing years, and now we find to our surprise that the relationship has been growing. Someone I only remember as a casual
acquaintance has become, I find, with the passage of time a
close friend. Sometimes, less often, one realizes sadly that
with the passing of the years the relationship has withered and
died. No longer do we share the same views, the same hopes
and fears. With mutual regret we accept that somehow,
somewhere, the roads have diverged, the lines of communication have been stretched and ultimately have broken down.
We meet now as relative strangers, finding that we belong to
different countries, scan different horizons, enjoy different
jokes, and to our contemporaries are seen as having taken on
different colours. We can become alienated from our culture,
our roots, and our faith, and even from those with whom we
were once intimate friends. A mother may alienate her child.
One has seen it happen too often.

The fear a mother has of losing her own may well, as most
mothers know, make her over-protective, and few would say
it can be easy to walk that tight-rope and train the child to
independence and maturity. Over-paternalism or undue
fragmentation can be equal problems facing any superior. To
develop and strengthen the ties of a love based on respect is to
try to do something where, above all, Mary the Mother of God
is the perfect example. But for every mother there is clearly a
path new every day, and maybe I should be exhorting her not
to miss these all-important moments whilst she worries about
a past beyond recall, and fears a future which is not yet and
may never be as bad as she suspects.

To live in the present, to appreciate the value of the present
moment, to take the opportunity of growing closer to her
children—and to each one in particular—in his or her present

stage: that seems to me a message I must try to get across. Why do we all try to live in the future when we are young, and in the past when we are old? Planning can be escapism from present commitments. The opportunity of the here and now can never be recovered, will never come again. The house depends on its foundations. Failure to enter into, to deepen and enjoy a relationship with the child at this age, or at that, means a permanent loss, a weakening of the foundation needed for later life. Hindsight teaches us this, but that is a sad way to learn, and does not repair the losses. Examples, sometimes horrific, spring to mind of young mothers thinking that when their children are at this or that particular age they can afford to cut down on the time they give them; and the poor parents, for this applies even more particularly to the fathers than to the mothers, realize too late that traumas and nightmares and all sorts of other disturbances and psychosomatic illnesses spring from what was a kindly meant, but ill-judged, loosening of the parental reins. Sometimes I have known parents who have traced what seems to be permanent damage to their young from their attempts to wean them before they were ready for it, and all of us will have met people permanently insecure and overwhelmed with a sense of inadequacy which would seem to be the result of a love-deficiency in their early life. But the children of Dee are inevitably going to suffer some loss because their father has deserted them, and how far can, or should, Dee try to make up for that deficiency? I can only urge her to be herself, and love her children so dearly that they will know that that strand can always safely withstand the strain of time.

(I wonder whether this accounts for what would seem to be similar difficulties which religious so often experience in later life: when they were young in the religious life were their superiors lacking in understanding, and perhaps unwilling to enter into a personal relationship? Were they insufficiently open, or human? I remember one wonderful man who in his old age was made a rector, and all the 'difficult' young men who had doubts about their vocation were sent to his house.

He was naturally kindly, and an extrovert who enjoyed life and liked people. He was fascinated by the men who came his way, not as cases which had to be helped, but as people in whom he was genuinely interested. One day, one of the young men told me that he was the first superior he had met who really wanted to know about, and if possible meet, his father and mother and brothers and sisters, and even his friends. I think probably that then, for the first time, that young man began to feel at home in the religious order to which he had dedicated his life.)

I do not think Dee or any mother would need this advice when their children are young, but it may be important when the children grow up and the child–mother relationship has to give way to a new relationship more akin to friendship.

III

Clearly a mother needs the wisdom of Solomon, and, if she has not got it, she will have to learn by experience like the rest of us, and for that she will need a certain amount of basic humility and a sense of humour. It has been said that the tidier the kitchen, the worse the meal. The good chef has to have in him something of the artistic temperament, and few artists have been renowned for their tidiness. A bit of this, a touch of that, a bubbling cauldron of invention always fresh and new-prepared for the occasion. No list of rules can produce a masterpiece—for that requires genius, and something of that same spirit of creativity is needed by the young mother. Like the chef she has to be infinitely adaptable; she has to face a new and ever-changing situation, she cannot rely on the recipes of the past. The success of yesterday, if slavishly reproduced today, can easily become a recipe for disaster. In every way I can, I must boost her morale and encourage her sense of self-sufficiency, which has inevitably taken such a knocking when her husband left her. Depression will be a problem which she will always have to be on her guard against.

Somehow the children have to be weaned, to be taught to shift for themselves, to become self-reliant. Just as in conversation the silences are often more important that what is said, so perhaps what is not done may be more important than what is done. We live in a topsy-turvy world. What we say is far more dependent on the tone of voice, the emphasis, the urgency or lack of it, the interest, than the logic and form of the sentence. Silence can be more expressive than a torrent of words. Real communication is between people, and not between their vocal organs and auditory systems. A child's drawings and scribblings may reveal far more than what he says or asks. His dependence may be shown not so much by his actions as his lack of actions, or his failure to respond. So often in human affairs we mean the opposite of what we say, and sometimes even the opposite of what we do. We know that the expressions 'industrial action', 'a strike', 'a work to rule', 'you've had it', all mean the opposite of what the words say. So too it is not surprising that 'I'm all right', 'O.K.', even 'no', can be cries for help which is apparently being rejected. We always expect to be understood ourselves, and it is curious that while we do not expect to be treated or taken logically at our face value, so often we seem to expect others, and especially children, to be less complicated and more easily intelligible than ourselves. Thank goodness most mothers, and certainly Dee, understand all this, and especially the value of silence, but I have known deserted mothers who were so lonely they could never stop talking, and had quite lost the ability to listen to anyone, perhaps especially to their own children.

A mother has to train her children to recognize the guidelines to happiness, to accept the laws of God; and perhaps she can learn something from the experience of the Church. It used to be said that when the Church defined a doctrine she tended to lose more than she gained; that a definition, rather than increasing our knowledge, detracts from it. It is a curious paradox, yet a definition is often a confession of failure. The absolute truth was, and always remains, more than can be expressed. By pin-pointing one aspect of truth the rest of the

truth becomes obscured, and can more easily get out of proportion. It is as though one tried to pour the whole jug of water
into a glass, and wasted almost more than one saved. Except of
course that the Church can, and over the ages has continued
to, restore the balance as it has been upset now by this heresy,
now by that. It seems to me that there is something of this
between parents and their children, and even between the
superior and his subjects; they are subject to the same human
limitations which the Church experiences when she tries to
teach her children. The Church has to lay down the laws from
time to time, but every law is again a confession of weakness,
and useless unless there is good will—and you cannot legislate
for that. St. Ignatius wanted his followers to be able to live
together without laws, and in saying that he was repeating
what every founder of a Religious Order has wished. St.
Ignatius hoped that the interior law of charity would be sufficient, but he realized quickly that, if men are to live together,
then ideals and means to the end have to be spelled out, the
lines of communication strengthened, and bridges built. So
too with the young parents. They have to lay down the law,
and yet inculcate a spirit which is not subservient to the law.
They have to prepare the ground for ties and loyalties, knowing that only the Truth can free them from fear. Unless their
own minds are clear they are unlikely to be able to teach their
children. I think Dee, a talented girl, can probably do this all
right on her own, and perhaps more easily without that husband who would have tended to dogmatize.

I remember one young teacher who, although fully trained
and an excellent artist herself, refused to teach. She could not
bear to cramp and distort the spontaneity of her young
charges. But somehow, they have to be taught. The adage that
the truths worth knowing are caught not taught is true
enough, and perhaps more widely appreciated by women
than by men. But in and through her attitude to the spirit
behind the law, and to the things worth knowing, the mother
has to deepen her ties with her children so that, united by
common hidden ideals, they may be helped to grow to matur-

ity. Perhaps if she could look towards the experience of the Church and see its failures as well as its successes over the ages she might be encouraged.

IV

But the enormity of such a task might well discourage Dee, so I suppose it would be useful to say something about what the theologians used to call 'gratia status'. By this they meant that God never asked anyone to do anything beyond his capability. However inadequate a man might feel, if he found himself with some particular task to perform then he could be sure (perhaps only if he asked) that he would be given the help necessary to fulfil his obligations. When one tries to look at it from the point of view of God it sounds pretty obvious. But not so easy from the point of view of Dee.

To understand the role one is being called upon to play is useful. Yet every role has to be tailor-made to fit our different personalities, talents and backgrounds. We can only hope to know the expectation of God for each one of us when we ourselves are at peace, and the hidden depths of our own hearts can be seen more clearly. More we cannot know, so for the most part we have to rest content to be working in the dark. Yet there is clearly a role, especially for mothers, and for them there are many rules and guide-lines. Whilst we would be foolish to follow them slavishly, we would be still more foolish to ignore them.

The danger is that, longing for security, we use labels instead of guide-lines; that we try to conform ourselves to our own preconceived image of what we think we should be. A cool hard look may be required, so that we can more realistically see what our status really is, and what we as individuals are being called upon to do.

Many a headmaster has told me how difficult it is to persuade parents that they need to deal with the child they have, not the one that in their heart of hearts they had hoped for. The preconceived image of what we expect from others can be no less damaging than trying to live up to false ideas of what we think God expects for each one of us.

Two heads are sometimes better than one, and the young mother on her own may find it difficult to stand back and see things in perspective. She is naturally inclined to leap at the first solution which presents itself. It is more difficult for her than for others to adopt what I would call the taxi-cab philosophy of life. If I take a taxi it is because I am in a hurry, and if I am in a hurry I cannot afford to argue about the cost—I have got to pay up. But if I can afford to wait, then I can nearly always win. Given time, most problems can be solved. But Dee has not got time on her side, she cannot afford to wait, she has got to act, and act now, but if I can I must warn her against accepting too easily any label. Any definition of a role, with its inbuilt hard lines, although it may capture one glimpse of the truth, will do less than justice to the beauty and infinite variety needed in a dynamic growing relationship.

I have rather 'gone on' about these relationships, because they are of the essence of human responsibility. I wonder how one would define a human person? Many over the ages have tried, and all the definitions reveal something of the ideals, the human aspirations of their composers. But somewhere in the final answer must be found the sum of the human relationships into which the human person has entered or has the potential to enter.

V

But what, I can hear my friends say, about Dee's social life? She needs adult company. Just as the student needs a change from his studies, and those compelled to lead the 'nine to five' life need the week-end and the summer holiday, so does the young mother need to get away from it all from time to time, so that she may be herself and see things in perspective. It is an argument as old as time, and would not have enjoyed such a good innings had it not had a germ of truth within it. I remember many years ago when going to teach in Leeds, a large industrial and at that time very smoggy city in the north-east, I was told, 'You are lucky. It has one great advantage; it is so easy to get out of it.' Escapism all along the line. Yet change has its value, and so does social life and adult friendships. But not only for the mother; the children equally need the companionship of their peers. They will get it at school, and they will need their friends at home too.

Amongst the poor in the old days in Liverpool, each street was a community of its own. Most streets had a 'posh' end, and a poorer end; most streets were either rather superior to the ones which crossed them, or slightly envious of them. There was a hierarchy not apparent to the casual observer or the newcomer, but important in the lives of the people. One resulting advantage was that, however poor the people were in this world's material goods, they were rich in their friendships and sense of community. They belonged, and knew it. Each street was a world of its own.

Of course, there was little privacy. Time and again you would meet the most frightful overcrowding. Despite this, in some houses everything was always neat and tidy and the children spick and span and happy. In other houses, the filth and stench would make one want to vomit, and the poor children obviously longed to escape. As always, you could meet all sorts within the compass of one short street.

It was all a question of the spirit, a question of morale, of guts, of motivation, of some inner urge which gave some of them hope and faith in themselves and in their family too, a faith and hope apparently denied to others. As Viktor Frankl showed, the human spirit can rise above the most desperate situations even in concentration camps, and anyone who has ever worked in the slums knows that many of the poor have had to contend with situations which have been unutterably demoralizing —that time and again one was privileged to meet the most wonderful people who rose above it all, but that many others —and who could blame them—succumbed into hopelessness.

Very clearly material wealth, or the lack of it, was not ultimately the most important fact which helped some families
not only to survive but even to prosper as families, whilst
others went under. The attitude to wealth and possessions,
and above all to people, was what really counted. It is the
spirit, and in the last analysis only the spirit, which really
matters. The rest is dross.

But if a mother has young ones, she still has to feed and
clothe and educate them. The Scriptures tell us that God saw it
was not good for man to be alone, and perhaps loneliness is
the greatest danger for the young mother on her own. Loneliness, like fear, is a bad counsellor, and has to be confronted.
Like every other young mother, the mother on her own will be
asked to help others more unfortunate than herself; she will be
asked to help in the parish and in the school. Provided she has
good health, there is a world waiting for her if she has the
courage and can find the time to try to live up to her own
ideals, her own convictions, and her own ambitions.

When I was young I remember trying to get people to help
with various chores on the parish or amongst the parents. In
my ignorance I tended to ask those with no children to help in
the parish, and those with only one child to help in the school.
I quickly learnt my mistake. Those with the fewest possessions
are so often the most generous, the most compassionate and
understanding; and I learnt that it was the mother with a sick
husband and a huge brood of children who was always willing
to put herself out to help a good cause. I would think this is an
important lesson for the young mum to learn: the more she
gives, the more she has. Of course, Our Lord put it much
better than that. But the fact that what he said is true still comes
home to most of us faint-hearted believers with a shock not
perhaps so unlike what St. Thomas experienced when he met
the Risen Lord, and found that all he had said was really true,
not only in and for the world to come, but here and now. The
hundredfold. Sometimes you meet people overwhelmed with
the happiness of it, although from the point of view of this
myopic world they are poor and deprived.

VI

So I find myself coming inexorably back to my first conclusions. Somehow I must find ways and means of stirring up Dee's faith, of boosting her morale, of making her appreciative of the present, of countering the demon of depression. I know, and she in her heart of hearts knows, that the Holy Spirit does really want to stir up her faith, and this he can do in an infinite number of ways. But one way, which always seems to be a winner, is for her to help someone more deprived than herself. Just as the sick in Lourdes forget their own pains and problems and frustrations as they see other pilgrims suffering more than themselves; just as they long to help, and by helping others find they quite unexpectedly have helped themselves even more—so too, if only the young mother can just begin to appreciate the strength of her position, and use it to help others, her whole family will acquire a new dimension.

Because she has entered into the passion of Christ—albeit unwillingly—she has been called to a special work in the sanctification of the world. It is all like Judo. It is not a question of using one's own strength, but of seeing, accepting, loving, and using the reality of one's own position. Because she is poor, because she is deprived, because she has hardships greater than those around her, so she has very special graces, strengths, insights, and opportunities, of which her more wealthy and talented peers are deprived. Far easier for her to be open and frank—ah, that perhaps is something else one really ought to say something about. In her position she can really be herself. No need for a mask.

It is easy for self-pity to creep in. It is so easy to accept the smug pity with which the world around would try to drown her, as it has drowned so many with its false values. Unless she can not only accept the situation but see in it the kindly hand of God Our Father, she will lose much of that precious opportunity which is hers. Merely to 'accept' can lead to a sponge-like mentality which is the equivalent of death. That seems to be one of the real dragons on the way which devours many. Listless, without energy, without hope—what sort of values would such a mother give her children? Unless she has a vision and a dynamism and some humour with it all, her children are likely to grow up far from rounded. A defeatist, negative attitude would seem to be the subtlest of the evil forces which have destroyed so much of our civilization over the past few years, an attitude which, like a cancer, can grow unnoticed—and all because of a failure to respond to the *gratia status*, to the challenge of a responsibility, a failure to take a positive line. Somehow I must encourage her to rise above the immediate heartaches.

It is not new thoughts or new ideals or new visions which most of us need; rather, we need to be reminded of those we already have, so that they may be taken out of storage, or sometimes out of the nursery, dusted and polished, and become again the banners under which we are proud to serve. To see things freshly, as they really are, and always were, before our eyes grew clouded and the vision dim.

It may interest readers to see part of the reply which Dee sent me after I had drafted a letter on the lines I have already indicated.

'. . . it was nice of you to write such a long letter, but it was horribly serious. I know you wanted to help and I'm sure most of what you say is very true but the honest fact is that I get terribly depressed, life seems to go on and on and you never get a break which makes it frightfully dull, and despite the children—oh, what you say is very true—but even so I do find I get so lonely and all the time there is the unending drudgery of work, work, work, and trying to meet the bills. Do write again, but I think a funny story which would make me laugh would be more helpful—I rather think you'll agree . . .'

I replied shortly—'I do', and sent her a funny card. It was all I could do. Funny stories are far more difficult than moralizing. So much for that bit of musing!

4 Depression

I

A priest friend of mine used to live in an old Victorian presbytery in London. As a junior curate he had a basement room with only half a worm's-eye view of the world above. By crouching on the floor and squinting upwards, or by standing on a chair near the casement window and craning your neck, you could hope to catch a glimpse of the sky. You were disappointed. All you could see was the tall whitewashed wall of the basement area and the lower half of the old iron railings which flanked the pavement. If you were lucky you might see a small child's face peering down through the railings, but usually all you could see were the swiftly moving legs of the anonymous passers-by. Their faces, their identities were hidden.

In these conditions my friend and I tended to rely upon our ears. Just as we easily recognize the steps of those with whom we live, and can guess their moods from the way they talk, so too we found that the anonymous footfalls betrayed the moods of their possessors. Listening, in the nether regions, as in a submarine, was curiously revealing. With a tiny pinch, a mere soupçon, of imagination you could guess at the characters of the owners of the feet you heard above. As a child dresses up her dolls, investing each with a special personality, so did we clothe those footsteps like the *dramatis personae* in a play.

The rhythmic clickety-clack, almost military in its precision, revealed the owner intent upon the business of the day, with a zest for living. Probably young secretaries determined not to be late for work again today. The airy-fairy tread of the young lovers whose feet scarcely touched the ground; for them time long ago had ceased to matter. The dancing feet of children belonged to another world, a world of wonder and excitement all their own. Their feet invited us to share their joy, to return to that world we could no longer see. The slow shuffling feet of the very old passed by as if never to return.

Quite different were the dreary fitful heavy footfalls of the weary and depressed which seemed to dread the advent of yet another day. The fight of these people was clearly lost before their battle had begun. They could not see the world which filled the children with delight; alone, they had no loved one, and time dragged slowly by; the future held no challenge, only the certainty of yet another failure. The light had left their lives, the world weighed heavy on their shoulders, their feet faltered on their way.

We all know this sadness of depression as a disease which always threatens to eat, like a cancer, into our very souls, and destroy our zest for living. It is rampant in the world today. To control, curtail, and conquer its incursions lest we be overcome is all-important. This is indeed a basement area where life is still a warfare, and where defeat would be disaster. Depression is a matter where we are not without our own personal experience, and we have all suffered from its effects in others. We may be unable to provide a satisfactory definition, but we know it well enough to realize that sometimes it indicates a serious malaise which calls for expert medical treatment, at other times it is more like the common-cold: part of the normal lot of man.

We tend to blame the weather, not entirely without reason. Grey skies, low atmospheric pressure, and humidity are partly to blame, especially when they seem to unite with mental, economic, family, and social worries. Sorrows never seem to strike singly.

No wonder we, at the receiving end, get depressed. Others may show resilience and dissolve disasters with a laugh. Most of us find this impossible. One small consolation I experience is the knowledge that depression can never again be quite as wretchedly hopeless an experience as it was when I suffered it in my teens. Probably other more mature people get this sense of futile, helpless depression more frequently in later life. But when we are young, especially between seventeen and twenty-two, the future looks not unlike the distant mountains in a hilly part of Wales. There, it used to be said, if you can see the mountains it is a sure sign of approaching rain; if you cannot see them, it is because it is already raining. So I think we felt sometimes about depression when we were young—it was never very far away, and could and did descend without warning, like the misty rain in Wales; and then it blotted out the landscape.

The young see life in starker contrasts than do those at any other stage of life, and have a greater zest for living and deeper emotional involvements. Inevitably they are more vulnerable than the old and sere. Their insights carry greater penetrative power, but their resilience and ability to compromise and adapt are still untried; they can more easily be broken. When the future is uncertain, and it is impossible to know where life is leading, where it should lead, or where one would like it to lead, no wonder they sometimes feel confused. Emotional problems, like falling in and out of love, complicate the issues.

I well remember a girl telling me that she had found being eighteen the most difficult time of her life. I think she was probably very normal. She despaired of finding a suitable young man, or a life which would satisfy her deepest longings. She was not then old enough to be able to look back on a past already lived to encourage her to face the uncertainties of the future. Another told me how miserable she had been at the university which she attended. She had lived on the campus, and had been deprived of all real contacts with the young and old. She found she was without those outlets her temperament needed for affection, mother-love, hero-worship and worthwhile responsibility for others.

One young man I remember twice attempted suicide. He was slightly older than most of the other students, and felt life was passing him by. He had no girl-friends at that time, and was not very clever. He had come up to university the hard way. The thought of a long, deadly, monotonous life, similar to what he was then experiencing, stretching out ahead of him in time, was too much. Subsequently he became a Catholic, and his faith gave him a philosophy of life which enabled him to see how things, given time, really do fit together. He married and had children, and although his life was hard in that his working day was always long and his job gave him little satisfaction, he managed to become the leading figure in the ecumenical movements in the village where he lived. Everyone loved and admired him, and he made many friends. Life turned out to be quite different from what he had feared. Alas, he died young, but he achieved much. His life could so easily have been wasted, and many people whose lives were enriched by his sympathy and understanding would have been the poorer. His intense depressions as a younger man enabled him in later life to enter into the hearts and minds of others in a way given to few.

Sometimes depression leads to 'contracting out'. I was surprised when I was first called to a house where the man refused to get out of his bed. He was too depressed to do anything. He was not ill, nor did he claim to be. He just lay in bed and expected his wife to bring his meals and get him more novels from the local library. He lived in a world of fantasy. Talking to my probationer friends I found that at the time, shortly after the war, this was not uncommon. The motherly instinct of the poor wife was so strong that she was content to slave away, and would not co-operate in the strong-armed solutions I suggested. We never solved that problem.

The young who are unemployed or under-employed inevitably feel an enhanced sense of insecurity and inadequacy. Through no fault of their own, they find they are considered a burden on their family, and perhaps even on the local community. No wonder they react violently, becoming sometimes intolerably arrogant, self-assertive, and cocksure, and contradicting even their parents in public, as if they enjoyed embarrassing them. Sometimes they become morose, moody and silent; at other times they take delight in being 'difficult' and unwilling to co-operate in normal daily jobs about the home. Apparently selfish and inconsiderate to those whom they really love deeply, whose help they need and want, and yet they apparently take pleasure in rejecting this help. It is a condition we all know well. They are desperately unhappy, and all their apparent 'tantrums' are really a cry for help.

Help should be given, but not by words. Occasions are necessary where they can show their love, and be sure it is both needed and will not be rejected. They do not realize that their parents also yearn for their affection. A baby brother or sister is the perfect solution which nature sometimes provides in a large family. Affection and love can be safely given to those who clearly long for it, and in so doing personal problems are forgotten and the true self found. Their problems are solved, at least for the moment, because someone needs them. Helping in a Cheshire home, or with the handicapped, or in an orphanage, or pushing a trolley in a home for the dying, and in countless other ways, the young can find deep satisfaction. They often too find friendships which last through life.

The old, the sick, small children, and the handicapped provide the young with an opportunity to reassure themselves and, they hope, others that they are willing and able to assume responsibility in society. With increased self-assurance they become free, and can more easily find the friends and the jobs they need. Once they experience some measure of security, they no longer have to assert themselves and prove themselves on every unsuitable occasion. Their loneliness is gone. Who was it who said that he found the London Underground during the rush-hours the most lonely experience in a long life, whereas others find it an exciting experience? So much depends upon our mental attitudes, and what we expect from people. Experience is a help.

II

Whilst life in the twenties is certainly preferable to what it was in the late 'teens, life in the thirties is infinitely preferable. Indeed I find that life, like good wine, improves with every decade. It may lose some of its early sweetness and sparkle, and can become over-dry and even acid; but time gives it a richness, flavour, and bouquet which I would not wish to miss.

Alas, all would not agree. Depression sometimes hits the middle-aged, perhaps less violently, but often for more prolonged periods, than it hits the young. Disillusionment, a sense of failure, or a recognition of the futility of success adds to their troubles. Sometimes they realize too late that they have dedicated their lives to a worthless cause; they kicked and pushed their way through life, and climbed the greasy pole marked 'success', and now discover it was all a waste of time. The knowledge that they have squandered their opportunities, that they seem destined to be life's misfits, that their work, or their marriage, or the way they have brought up their children, has been a great mistake, takes the heart out of them. What can one say to those who have apparently, on their own reckoning, wasted their lives? No wonder they are depressed. How and where can they find joy, satisfaction, fulfilment, interior peace? Often they are no longer free; some of their commitments drag them down, and seem likely to destroy them. Like the young and the old, they are often obsessed by worry. They should, I think, be encouraged to be objective, and to identify if they can the root cause or causes of their troubles. If causes can be identified, perhaps they can be cured or dealt with—in which case all that is needed is courage.

But if the solution is not within their grasp? Then at least it becomes clear that worry is a waste of time. If I have failed to ensure that my tyres are at the right pressures when travelling at a sustained high speed, then I have plenty of cause to worry. The remedy is in my hands. But when I am forty thousand feet above the Atlantic, there is little I can do, unless I am the pilot, so why should I worry? Too late now to worry about my failure to fulfil my responsibilities which I should have dealt with earlier. There comes a time when all I can do is to commit myself and all my unfulfilled responsibilities into the hand of God. Prior to that moment worry will not help, but action will.

It can be helpful to set one's worries down on paper. If they are fantasies of the imagination, they vanish when confronted. If they are rooted in anxiety, maybe a visit to the doctor is called for. It may not be cancer or incipient blindness which is troubling me, but it is as well to know, and knowledge is far less crippling than uncertainty and fear of the unknown.

Worry, like scruples, is a disease of which we can become inordinately fond. It is no substitute for action, and it adds to our depression.

Often, especially in middle age, we are conscious of our failure to relate with people, especially with those whom we love, and this can easily lead to depression. The same principles always apply. Is there anything I can do to improve or restore the wished-for situation? If there is, then I should do it. If nothing can be done I need to face that fact, and turn my face to the future. This is where my Christian hope should help to give me the courage I may need to begin again.

Often, if we are realistic, we have to admit that the causes of depression can be physical. Too many late nights, too much drinking, too little self-discipline in our lives can all create a situation where the old-fashioned dose of salts or its equivalent is really the answer. Sometimes a spiritual purging, like a short week-end retreat, or a day of recollection, or a time apart by myself, without even a dog or a transistor, may help to restore the balance.

I was told that when unmarried girls living in bed-sits met in New York their first question would be: 'How good is your security?', in London they would ask: 'What do you pay?', whereas in Leningrad or Moscow the first question was 'How much footage have you got?' An English girl I knew well told me that in Russia it was almost impossible ever to be alone. She loved the Russians and enjoyed their company, but sometimes felt she needed to be alone. Late at night she would go to the cemetery, for this was the only time and place where she found it possible to be free to commune with herself. Unless the middle-aged can sometimes be alone and face themselves, their groundless—or perhaps well-grounded—fears will grow apace and be dealt with less effectively. All through our lives we have to create the opportunities we need so that we can be true to ourselves.

III

Like the common cold, sometimes we can feel depression coming. We should then rush for our bottle of spiritual vitamin C, and fight it off early before it gets a grip of us. I was much impressed by the basic common sense in a new hospital where every woman patient who had surgery was offered a 'hair-do' free of charge if she went for it within a day or two of the operation. Encouraged to get up quickly, she found her self-confidence also restored; depression was countered before it had begun. One is always led to understand that new hats produce the same effect. Idiosyncrasies may vary. A foreign lady I knew was miserable in England because there was no wine on the table. She did not drink; but she associated wine with happiness within the family, for so it had always been in her own home. The absence of what we normally take for granted can depress us without our understanding the cause;

whilst little unexpected joys can lift us out of ourselves and keep us better balanced. The middle-aged, faced with redundancy or early retirement, need more than little things, important though they are, if they are to face the future with equanimity.

Perhaps it is worth while to pursue a little further the comparison between the common cold and depression. Colds tend to hit us when we are already down, at a low ebb, with our resistance weakened. We have all known those who were too busy to be ill. They could not afford the time. Nurses, doctors, those with a family business or a position of special responsibility, may find that their temperature soars at the week-end when they are free to relax, but it will go down again on Monday morning in time for them to take up once again the responsibilities which are so much a part of their life. For others, for whom their work is a drudgery, impersonal and boring, a time to be filled in until the week-end comes, illness will strike on Monday, but by Friday they will be well again in time for what they really want. We have all met people who have forgotten their illness when faced with a sudden emergency or some unexpected and very pleasurable event; the sudden flow of adrenalin, or some other undisclosed factor, enabled them to throw it off.

What is the motivation which can produce similar effects in the middle-aged so that, forgetting the past, they will face the future with zest? The sudden challenge of a bull has caused people to jump over six-foot walls in order to escape; the tireless urging of a loving wife has led great men to overcome what could have been disaster. By being encouraged to talk to someone they trust, many have acquired the strength they needed to accept the challenge of the unknown future which lies ahead. The situation needs to be confronted, or it will destroy the peace and happiness of the home. The old life has ended and a new one must be begun; new sources of energy must be found—and where better than from their family, the children and grandchildren, and all their friends?

Most of us know men and women who have not been able to

surmount that crisis and have withdrawn into themselves, and then the added problems of loneliness and bitterness have been added to their miserable lot. Bridges need to be built, and communications established. Sometimes we meet men and women who, in their deep depression, have built castles to protect their inner sanctum. Seriously wounded in the past, at least in their imaginations, thinking themselves rejected by society, feeling threatened and unwanted in the present, they have built high walls, thick and well-nigh impregnable, behind which they take cover. The embrasures are filled with cannon which delight in firing on friend and foe alike; if boiling oil were available it would cheerfully be dispensed on all, and the pure clean air is for ever full of their complaints about the cruel lot of man. It is a far cry from Job sitting so patiently on his dung-heap, especially when their depression seems to be fed on self-pity and bitterness, with no room for faith or hope or joy. No wonder that sometimes those wonderful wives and daughters, and sometimes those wonderful husbands and sons, who look after such people tend themselves to get depressed. It is a contagious business.

The practical solution must surely be to build a bridge, maybe a funny steep hump-backed old bridge; but somehow, on some level, real communication must be established before the inner citadel can be stormed. A friend of mine, faced with the problem of how to help a very lonely and miserable old farmer, discovered he was an authority on pigs. My friend read up sufficient to be able to ask a few intelligent questions. Like most lonely men the farmer craved an audience; my friend listened patiently and returned frequently, and found he had acquired not only a friend but even the beginning of a real interest in breeding pigs. I'm not sure how the farmer fared, but the outer defences at least were down. Sometimes I suspect that an interest in football, horses, or beer, may have come from a similar good intention to provide a bridge of friendship with someone shut in on himself.

On top of one of the mountains near Katmandu there lives a holy hermit. Every day a local farmer arranges for food and drink to be brought near enough for the hermit to come and get it. There is an old iron bridge made in Scotland which was brought from somewhere, and which now crosses one of the ravines and saves many hours on the road which really leads to nowhere. But for the old hermit that bridge makes a world of difference.

IV

Even though outer defences crumble and a friendship based on a common interest is established, the inner citadel of the heart in which so much depression wells up may remain closed. We all know people who will talk and talk in order to avoid talking at a deeper level—they fear silence and the personal involvement which ensues. Left to themselves they rush back home and hug their bitterness and depression to their hearts. What can one do to help? Sometimes they torture themselves over some real or imagined slight. Their pride is hurt. Only love and friendship can produce a cure.

Sometimes a sense of guilt is the cause, and the cure is clear. The truth must be faced, confronted, and the present situation can then be accepted and life can begin again. This may well need the help of a good confessor or a skilled psychiatrist; the guilt complex has to be dissolved, and the faults and failures of the past accepted, so that they can become a source of strength. The Church speaks of past forgiven sin as a *felix culpa*, a happy fault, for now it is a stepping-stone to God and a further claim upon his infinite mercy. The more realistic we are and the more we face the facts, the stronger we become.

> I am the vine,
> you are the branches.
> Whoever remains in me, with me in him,
> bears fruit in plenty;
> for cut off from me you can do nothing.

A divided conscience which reflects an interior conflict

always destroys our peace of soul and is a cause of disquiet. Once we are over that problem, the root cause may have to be dealt with and new habits will have to be formed. If we are to live with our past, not as a skeleton safely locked away in a cupboard but as part of our present which makes us what we are, then we may need the courage to display it. Not necessarily to everyone, but certainly to God, and sometimes as the case may demand to our family and close friends. The reformed alcoholic who is prepared to admit that he suffered from the disease of alcoholism and is now cured can, by his very openness, do far more to help others than he would be able to do if he kept his own background secret. The decision of how open to be, and with whom, rests with him.

I knew a man who had a very short temper. He would lose it frequently and quite violently. The storm never lasted long. He was always repentant and would afterwards apologize sincerely. He knew his failing, and it became a source of strength because he was humble enough to recognize it himself. Old habits die hard, and the danger is that we become fond of them and excuse them to ourselves, and cease to try to master them. We can become just as addicted to depression as others do to smoking, drinking, and drugs. The real danger is that we may cease to want a cure, and inevitably, because the *malaise* is deeper and the causes come from without as well as from within, depression is not easily overcome.

The well-known story of St. Catherine of Siena may help. She had been suffering from incessant temptations and was depressed. She complained to Our Lord, 'Why did you leave me all alone; it was almost more than I could bear,' and she heard the answer, 'You were never alone, I was in your heart giving you strength to endure and conquer.' It was so similar to what the Apostles had experienced during the storm at sea. Apparently they were depressed because they had been sent away across the lake to row home in the evening whilst Our Lord had stayed on a mountain to pray. A storm arose. The Apostles were not all fishermen, and some of them were unused to such conditions. Suddenly Our Lord appeared walking on the water and they shrieked with terror. They thought he was a ghost. Very often we are faced with some experience which we will see in retrospect as a grace from God, but we regret it because it does not fit into the pattern of life which we are weaving for ourselves.

Naaman always seems to me to be a good example of a happily married man who nevertheless had plenty of cause for depression. When G.O.C. to the King of Syria, and at the height of his career, he was struck with leprosy. He must have been a decent man, for the little Jewish slave girl whom he had captured on one of his earlier expeditions clearly liked him enough to tell his wife about the great prophet in Israel who could cure him. The story is well known of how he followed her advice, and was told by the prophet to wash seven times in the Jordan. He was furious. His career was already in jeopardy. He thought his request for help had merited better treatment; but far from being treated with the solemnity which he had expected in so serious a matter, it had been dealt with almost light-heartedly and with scant ceremonial. You can almost see him grumbling to himsetf. Like most of us, he was a practical man and liked reason to govern his life. What was so special about the waters of the Jordan? His friends came to his rescue, and pointed out that if something stupendous had been demanded he would willingly have done it—why not then do this little simple thing? He did, and was cured. His whole life must have taken on a new quality which, but for that trial, it would never have acquired.

Sometimes our friends, and sometimes strangers, may step in to rescue us in our perplexity. The Ethiopian eunuch, on his way home after a pilgrimage to Jerusalem, could not understand the prophet Isaiah, and Philip was sent to help him. 'Do you understand what you are reading?' he asked. 'How can I,' replied the eunuch, 'unless I have someone to guide me?' So he invited Philip to get in and sit by his side. Now the passage of Scripture he was reading was this:

> Like a sheep that is led to the slaughter-house,
> like a lamb that is dumb in front of its shearers,

like these he never opens his mouth.
He has been humiliated and has no one to defend
  him.
Who will ever talk about his descendants,
since his life on earth has been cut short.

So often our worries about the future are groundless. If the blood of the martyrs is the life-seed of the Church because they are baptized into Christ's death, then all those trials which seem to indicate death to all our hopes are an invitation to share, joyfully, in Christ's work. What greater favour could he give us?

5 Insight

LIKE the blue flash of the kingfisher darting down the Cherwell, gone before we knew he was there; leaving only a nostalgic memory, less than a half-forgotten dream which warms and somehow sweetens the summer air.

The cheering chime of the village clock at midnight; the clanking of the trains in the still of the night, and then the sudden morning chorus of the birds heralding the dawn.

The first smile in a child's eye, the scent of the trees in spring, giving us glimpses of hidden worlds and conjuring up the past with long lost memories of days gone by.

There are so many moments with overtones which cannot be recaptured, nor ever quite forgot. They speak to us in the secret places of our heart. Inspirations? They are insights into the magic of the present moment, and point to a world we sometimes take for granted and can no longer see.

The drops of water on the silver birch glistening in the morning sun as though the whole tree was shimmering with an inner radiance. It was said of Rouault that in early life he was apprenticed to a maker of stained glass, and in later life as an artist he was always looking for the light burning behind the picture, a light peeping through now here, now there, transfusing the lights and shadows with an inner glow. As the setting sun casts its spell over the white fleecy clouds and sets them all on fire as though with a radiance all their own, so does the grace of God ever give us new insights into the world around us. The magic depths are there for all to see.

The secrets remain hidden when the water is ruffled by the wind and we are too close to see beneath the dark, opaque moving surface; but on a still summer's evening from a nearby mound the clean translucent water of a mountain lake, like a pane of glass, reveals the secrets of the depths below.

During the storm, the hard rain strikes our faces and, as we fight for breath, we cannot smell; but after the storm is over, the sweet scents of grass and roses, lilac, thyme, heather and gorse and pine-trees and the freshness of all living things fills the air we breathe. At such times our senses become alive and grow perceptive to what we never saw or smelt before.

There are many fleeting moments when our darkness is lit up by the reflected glory of the setting sun as it brings out the warm hidden honey colour of the Cotswold stone, and in the peace and quiet of the evening we smell the scents we've missed but had forgotten all through the long working day.

Things are never just what they seem. The magic of new insights draws us further on, and when our night is lit by the flash of lightning we see the lifelines holding, though our faith seem dead and God hidden far away.

At such moments we may feel like George Herbert:

Who would have thought my shrivell'd heart
Could have recovered greenness? it was gone
Quite underground, as flowers depart
To feed their mother-root when they have blown;
Where they together
All the hard weather,
Dead to the world, keep house unknown.

These are thy wonders, Lord of power,
Killing and quick'ning, bringing down to hell
And up to heaven in an hour;
Making a chiming of a passing bell.
We say amiss,
This or that is:
Thy word is all, if we could spell.

The woods so dead in winter with all life hidden and unseen; and then the new hope with the first signs of spring. The tremulous yet radiant sheen of green, the early buds; the fore-shadowing of a fullness which is not yet but will be when the whole world will be carpeted with the glory of God. Meanwhile 'together All the hard weather', 'Dead to the world', we 'keep house unknown', unseen, and all seems dead.

So throughout God's creation where life is deeply hid. Our speech betrays us, and shows forth whence we came; a witness to life within us, and to our roots in times long past and in many other places. Now we see the father, now the mother, in he son. A look, a gesture, long before he speaks or even smiles, brings back the memory of one we loved, long dead or gone away.

We find that all things when we look more closely portray like shadows an unseen presence in the heart of things. That hidden, central, nodal, unseen point evokes, like songs on the summer air, like footsteps in the darkness of the night, like shadows cast by a flickering fire on the walls of some old building, and like footsteps in the sand, the knowledge that there is a Presence with us who works unseen and we keep house together. Our hearts are warmed, we know not how, by the mysterious Stranger in our midst. We find that when our senses, hearts, and head are gently idling, they are perceptive to a beauty everywhere which, like a bell, tells of his hidden Presence underlying and co-ordinating all things everywhere.

6 False gods

W HAT do you think about neat, tidy gardens? I mean the small ones which even an inexperienced gardener can handle. In Oxford we had such a garden which was always a mass of colour. A professional gardener came for a couple of hours once a week and kept everything tidy, trim, and beautiful. Then one day, alas, he decided he was young enough, a mere seventy, to work his passage—gardening—to Katmandu, which he had never seen, and where he had heard the scents and flowers are a constant joy. He wrote to me from Belgium and from Switzerland, full of happy contentment, interest, and even awe about the beautiful but very different gardens he had tended as he worked his way across Europe. He expects to be away three years.

Once he had gone, the flowers mourned and died; the colours went; the weeds came and the garden looked neglected and unkempt. It could not wait. The unskilled toiled and moiled too, but were unable, with twice the labour, to reproduce half the glory which had gone. I think it was the colour we missed most. What makes the English garden a delight through the short, drab, dark, dreary days of winter are not only the sharp skeletons of the trees, sketched in the evening light, but the contrasting shapes and shades. From our garden the charm had gone for ever, so it seemed, with our gardener on his way to Katmandu.

In the Middle Ages artists, and spiritual writers too, depicted the beauty of the garden of the soul, a garden enclosed, safe from the world, carefully tended, formal and predictable, like a picture postcard, with well-trimmed hedges, or high red-brick walls, with wrought-iron gates, criss-crossing paths and bushes and beds all keeping their allotted place. Brilliant flowers ordered in straight lines, like guardsmen on parade, were framed by green grass contrasting with the yellow gravel paths.

Why did our ancestors so hate even colourful weeds? Was it hurt pride, or were they identified with sin? When the gardeners, with constant clipping, moulded the shrubs and bushes as a sculptor sculpts his stone into their concept of the beautiful, was this too seen as the triumph of mind over matter, or the successful introduction of order into a disordered world?

Over-formalized, over-tidy, vaunting man's mastery over nature—could one ever relax in such a garden? What is the norm by which one can judge the man-made garden more beautiful than the riot of colour and the enticing jungle of interlocking bushes and shrubs struggling for survival which always enchants small children and which nature, left to itself, would quickly have produced? So that the beauty may be seen, there has to be a happy mean. If we limit our horizons we may indeed achieve success for a time; but if, through over-concentration on the means, we lose sight of the end, if we exclude the infinite, then the majesty and mystery which alone can satisfy is lost.

Most newly-weds are faced with a not dissimilar problem. Proud owners of their first home, they can only hope, with difficulty and after many inevitable mistakes, to agree on those priorities which should govern our lives. In the long rows of terraced houses, built in the early part of this century, the 'front parlour', full of family photos and precious relics of the past, was always kept so tidy that it could only safely be used by very special visitors or on important occasions. Often this 'parlour-complex' would indicate a disease which, if left unchecked, could spread and destroy the home. But children usually prevented this from happening. Every parent with small or teen-age children knows that an open house, like an open garden, into which the children can freely bring their friends and in which they can walk and talk and play and sometimes even eat without a guilty eye upon the clock, is a home where friendships can mature and many hours be cheerfully spent. Or are they wasted? It all depends upon our order of priorities. Some sacrifice is needed, if worthwhile results are ever to be achieved. For our houses are but means to an end, and much that we might prefer has to be given up in order that they may subserve the needs of the family. Unless we make such sacrifices they will soon cease to be our homes and become our prisons. Then those who enter in will feel themselves fettered and confined. In such conditions happiness cannot easily break in.

The mythical librarian who objects when books are taken off the shelves because the symmetry is disturbed hinders that cause of learning to which he has dedicated his life, and is as absurd as the chef who would not want his masterpieces to be eaten. Yet the over-tidy mother or father can be irritated by the chaos which small children joyfully introduce, as it were in the twinkling of an eye, and often indeed with a twinkle in their eyes, into an otherwise well-ordered house. The parents may usefully reflect that their mastery of their cherished home is being challenged by a newcomer so that their former placid horizons may be noisily extended, and something of the infinite may enter more fully into their own lives.

The order which we rightly value can acquire a disproportionate importance in the garden, in the home, and in the office too. If everything has to be filed, if all correspondence is equally important, then priorities can safely leave the building until it collapses under the sheer weight of paper. So too in all other walks of life, and even in a game of chess—where each piece has its own limited power and the skill depends on using them aright—we have to make the right judgements. The insignificant pawn may win a game, so too may the sacrifice of the queen; it all depends upon the previous judgements which have determined the relative importance which should be given to the pieces which still remain on the board.

Each situation has to be judged anew from day to day upon its present merits. Consistency, tidiness, and efficiency have places of their own, but woe betide us if we turn them into gods or rigid principles which we allow to dominate our lives.

I fear that these half-baked truths, which seem to me so clear and so importnt for the happiness of men and women living in a frenzied world, may sound banal and come from an empty head; but I would like to pursue them further, as they are important even within our own spiritual lives.

For if the half-wild garden full of weeds has a glory of its own, though not what we would really like to see, and if our house can easily cease to be our home, and if our office can become so neat and tidy as to preclude all personal contributions or creative work from the staff, then something very similar can happen within our own spiritual lives. Self-discipline, order, work, punctuality are helpful means, but easily become most cruel and demanding gods.

It is difficult to see much 'order' in the short public life of Christ. He seems to have been always available, his life dictated by the needs of others, so that sometimes there was no time to eat, at other times he was almost mobbed by the crowds, and times for prayer had to be snatched out of the deep watches of the night: 'He spent the night in prayer'. He could follow no daily, orderly schedule. The goal was clear; the means an ever-changing compromise with the daily demands made upon him. Only his love put order into what would otherwise have been a most disorderly affair. The order has to come from our own hearts, and sometimes it can get no further, at least for a little time.

I well remember a tutor I once had who, during the war, was sent to South America. I dreaded to think what the precise, well-ordered, staid, charming, Anglican Oxford don would make of the vibrant colourful life we associate with South America. I need have had no fears. Three years later he returned enraptured by what he had seen and heard. 'In this country', he exclaimed, 'we have lost the art of living'—and I think at that time he felt bitterly that he had wasted much of his life. Within a few months, however, old habits reasserted themselves, and so far as I could see he settled back quite happily into his old way of life.

But his example stimulated me to reflect that in most of us, born and bred in the pre-war era in an over-formalized society, where personality cults were suspect, there is a puritanical streak which often underlies otherwise superficially admirable qualities, and which tends to turn us into workaholics. We smugly feel that we are the better because we work so hard. Personal pleasure is regarded as self-indulgence; self-fulfilment or creative activities are looked on with suspicion and a slightly jaundiced eye. In short, many of us feel we are the better if we allow work to dominate our lives, whereas those born and bred in Catholic cultures more probably get their priorities better balanced when they would reverse these values. The poor commuters condemned to waste so many precious hours in travelling to and from the factory or office which dominate their lives have no alternative if they are to provide for their wives and children. One cannot blame them. But the system, readily accepted by so many out of economic necessity, may indicate an imbalance deeply rooted in our society which also affects many other aspects of our way of life.

The fanatic gardener who can never relax over tea in the garden because there is a weed here, or twig there, which offends his critical eye; the house-proud mother who can never relax and enjoy her home because there is something which should be done; my friend who escaped his tidy life for three blissful years before his roots drew him back to the habits of his childhood—all illustrate the dangers of this cult of so-called Efficiency. It is a cult which leads to the subsequent ruination of the enjoyment of simple pleasures, and a quite extraordinarily ruthless subordination of one's time to the inexorable demands of the clock. Surely the emphasis on 'saving time' which leads to so many hours being wasted is one of the great paradoxes of our day. The clock, a useful servant, is a cruel master.

Africa and most of the Middle East have, I am told, resisted its incursion, but in Europe only Ireland and some of the Mediterranean countries, and, until recent times, Malta, have remained immune to its blandishments. Perhaps a blue sky and a Celtic temperament helps one to keep one's perspectives better balanced. Surely the Irish attitude to time—'When God made time he made plenty of it'—may not help efficiency, may sometimes be exasperating, but is fundamentally sensible and sane.

7 Personal choice

I

MANY years ago, before traffic lights, windscreen wipers, and white lines had been invented, it was a delight to drive down the quiet English country roads. In those days it was comparatively easy to find the idyllic picnic place where the children could play and the old people have a quiet snooze after their lunch or tea. It is a different story today. Most of us know the exasperation which continual disappointment brings as we drive on and on looking for a suitable place to stop. The high kerbs, the steady flow of traffic, the wire fences, and the yellow lines make it almost impossible to find the wood or little copse, or the road into a field where we can pause, pull off the road and eat in peace and quiet. Sometimes we do, quite unexpectedly, see just what we want. Round Aldershot or on the south coast of Devon we may find ourselves in the most beautiful unspoilt countryside where the woods, the heather, or the virgin heath seem to offer us the perfect retreat where we could spend an hour or two undisturbed. We would do no one any harm. But when we are about to stop, nearly always we see those most unfriendly signs: 'Keep Out', and underneath we read 'Danger, Unexploded Bombs'. The army has been there before us, and we need no further warning. For the most part we obey such signs, and continue sadly on our lawful business. Life and limb may easily be endangered by ignoring the 'Keep Out' signs posted by the army, but much more is always certainly destroyed when we cross the boundaries marked out by God.

In an over-permissive society, this seems to be a truth we need to underline. For most of our contemporaries, all boundaries and hard lines are looked on with disfavour, and our choices are considered free unless the law, society, or convention judge otherwise. As a Christian I cannot agree. There are fixed boundaries within which we are free, but there are danger signals too where the 'Keep Out' signs are clearly posted for our good. However laudable and honourable our intentions, however attractive it may seem to ignore the prohibition, however special the pleading in which we indulge, the result of ignoring the commands of God is inevitably the same. We go behind something far worse than the Iron Curtain, into a slavery from which of ourselves there can be no escape. Far worse than having our lunch among the unexploded bombs.

But within the boundaries marked out by faith there is much room for the proper exercise of our freedom of personal choice. Our decisions may sometimes be less free than we think, for we are all the children of our age. Our foibles, and those pet loves and hates which we unconsciously learnt at home, can rule us and dictate our judgements. It may help us to consider two very different types of men: each one will judge any given situation instinctively and each may be right or wrong, but their judgements are seldom as free from those prejudices, pet hates and loves and foibles as they would like to think.

The one instinctively will always want to say 'yes', like the son in the Gospel who said he would go, but did not. The other is the cautious man, perhaps over-prudent, more conservative or realistic, and knows his limitations. His instinctive reaction will be to say 'no' until he has had time to reflect. The former tends to be more positive, sympathetic, open to new suggestions and to the work which may be involved; starry-eyed, he does not count the cost; an enthusiast, he may fall into the pitfalls round his feet, but he will always encourage. More attractive to most of us than the other, apparently so negative; so critical, refusing to get personally involved until he knows all the facts, he makes no rash promises; he does not let you down, but he cramps your style. Apparently so tied to the present that he has no time for the future. From his Olympian heights he always counsels caution (this may, of course, sometimes be due to a hardening of the physical arteries of his body, especially after a stroke, or in old age when lack of physical strength only allows accustomed paths to be safely followed), whereas his counterpart would say with St. Augustine the often misinterpreted phrase:

Love, and do what you want.

Most of us think we know our own limitations and favourite prejudices, but perhaps we do not sufficiently reflect that by giving in to them we merely harden our attitudes. Just as when we drive into the countryside we are free to go where we want, but for the most part, left to ourselves, we choose the places we most like and the routes we prefer. We like to think our own thoughts reasonably undisturbed. We value our freedom to make our own decisions, and only rarely do we realize that we usually exercise that freedom so that we may remain within the habits, customs, ruts, and routes where we are most at home.

We tend to admire those who sacrifice their freedom in order to help others, like the charitable person who goes off on his own selected route to take a weary hitch-hiker where he wants to go. Nuns and those who sacrifice their freedom in order to dedicate their lives to the needs of others used to be universally admired even by those who did not share their faith. Today such dedication is less highly regarded, and commitment is often discounted as almost a dirty word, involving as it does the focusing of one's sight upon a limited objective. By such activities we expose ourselves to the charge that we have chosen to become narrow, and prejudiced, and are no longer open to the viewpoints and opinions of others. In a sense this is true. But without some measure of commitment nothing worthwhile can be achieved. We see this in medical research, we know it is true of all great artists, and we expect it from those engaged at a professional level in any sport. Where there is international competition, or serious challenge with the elements, or in some areas of research, distinction can only be achieved by serious—sometimes lifelong—commitment. We have to back our hunches as to what is worthwhile; we need faith in our ideals if our principal occupations are to give us any satisfaction.

II

Since we are free, we should respect the rights of others too to choose their own routes through the maze of life. More often than we think they need our encouragement to pursue their own secret or unformed ambitions, and too often we can by a thoughtless remark dampen their incipient enthusiasms.

I remember one young man who wanted to become a writer. He was told by his friends that he should read the classics, that he should concentrate on English literature, that he must master Macaulay, and should avoid reading detective novels which would ruin his style. Whatever he produced was criticized as poor in quality compared with the great masters. Not surprisingly, he became discouraged and lost confidence in his own latent abilities. Alas, he had not learnt, and probably never did, that it is important to keep our dreams and visions to ourselves until they are sufficiently developed to withstand the hostile criticisms of well-meaning men. If we expose our ambitions and half-formulated ideas to the public gaze too soon, they are almost inevitably destroyed by those who have not yet begun to grasp the importance which we attach to them. Unable to share our vision, blind to the hidden beauty whch only we can see, our friends can easily demolish something which could have been important in our life. It is as though unwittingly they assist in the abortion of our unborn child. In a similar way within the unformed piece of stone an embryonic Michelangelo may be able to discern a great work of art. We should not blame others for not sharing in our vision. Advice, like criticism, is seldom geared to the concrete situation. More often it resembles that blanket bombing which was rightly decried after the war because it devastated whole areas, instead of limiting itself to the military objective. So, too, much criticism is often destructive, and too freely given. The tag of which Pope John was so fond is a good guide-line to what we need throughout our lives: 'In necessariis, unitas; in dubiis, libertas; in omnibus, caritas.' (In necessary matters, unity; in doubtful matters, liberty; in all things, charity.)

Sometimes, of course, we meet a man who has everything well planned out. He knows exactly where he wants to go, and what he wants to do. He is like that careful driver who has selected his route after listening to the news, and has taken care to avoid those places where long hold-ups of the traffic are to be expected. He has done his homework before setting off on his journey; his car is tanked up and all is ready for the expedition. We can admire his careful preparation, but most of us, who are uncertain of our destination or the best route, have to make further inquiries as we proceed on ou way. We have to accept conditions which are not of our own choosing, and make the best of them. I am often reminded of a friend of mine who thought it a great privilege to be allowed to make his own decisions and to stumble happily through life in the direction he had chosen, at his own pace, in a way intelligible to himself, free to do things badly. He was a well-rounded personality.

Another priest I knew was always willing to help others at a moment's notice and on any occasion with a sermon, an article, a retreat, or a talk. He was in great demand. Only rarely did he have the time to do himself justice, but he was not concerned with that. He produced a vast amount of writing and lectures and talks over the years and much, as he himself would have agreed, was only second-rate. But it was the best he could do within almost impossible conditions. He seldom hit the headlines until late in life, but by then it was apparent that he was a holy man who was prepared to sacrifice himself in the cause of helping others. I would not wish to give the impression that he was slapdash. He simply accepted the hard realities of a given situation, and did the best he could within those constricting circumstances.

A lesser man, a perfectionist, would have refused to do many of the things which my friend preferred to do badly rather than leave the work undone. My friend worked on the famous principle of G. K. Chesterton, that if a thing is worth doing, it's worth doing badly, and though he tried to do things well this was not always within his power. He had one principle which motivated his decisions: the desire to help his fellow men now—and as a result there was in him a quality, finer than anything he wrote or said, which communicated itself to others.

We have to make our own decisions, conscious that these decisions, far more than what we do or say, will determine the sort of being we become. 'We are what we are', or, if you prefer it, 'we are where we are' because of the judgements we have made. Too often the perfectionist, seeking a far distant goal, makes less headway than the lesser man who courageously commits himself to the needs of the present moment.

III

Unable to gaze into our own personal crystal ball to see where we should go or what we should decide, we can look back over our lives, long or short, and see how they have their individual pattern; that many different experiences and many different judgements—good and bad—have like a jigsaw come together and fashioned our life more and more into a whole. The process will, I like to think, remain incomplete on this earth, but go on and on for all eternity—being formed and fashioned into the likeness of Christ who is God as well as Man.

We can learn something from the past. Just as in our expedition into an unknown countryside we have to trust in maps, our hunches and a bump of direction and even the position of the sun, so too in our daily judgements we need help. Looking back we can see how vitally important it has always been that we trust God. It will be so in the future too.

> O Lord, it is you who are my portion and cup;
> it is you yourself who are my prize.
> The lot marked out for me is my delight:
> welcome indeed the heritage that falls to me!
> I will bless the Lord who gives me counsel,
> who even at night directs my heart.

As we reflect, we realize how our ideals have always needed regular reformulations, how we have often tried to force pieces into that jigsaw of our lives which did not fit there because, like a child, we were impatient and wanted them there at once. We can see now the frustration and unhappiness that would have ensued had we had our way; or maybe which did follow because we forced our own way on events because of our pet hates and loves and foibles. Sometimes we have been attracted, perhaps mesmerized would be more accurate, by the desire for economic security, for self-fulfilment, for marriage, for certainty, for independence, which we have substituted for God, so that we have gone off course, this way and that, zig-zagging through life; yet through it all the Holy Spirit has never been far away, helping us when we have been lost and even going round in circles. We all know the depression which descends upon us when we cannot find our destination. We waste much time and petrol looking for a house up in the hills when most sane people have long since gone to bed, and we experience equally frustrating moments when we are hurrying home along a road which we know well and find ourselves suddenly caught up in a traffic block because of an accident or road works, and so despite our efforts and our planning and furious driving we still arrive late at our destination.

In these conditions we need some of that morale which Sir Kenneth Wheare, in his funeral oration in St. Mary's Church in Oxford, attributed to Sir Douglas Veale:

He had such wonderful morale. Surrounded as he was in the Council and the Boards and the Delegacies and committees in the University by highly intelligent dons expert at criticizing whatever was proposed, eloquent in the expression of doubt and gloom, dedicated to the proposition that politics, or at any rate university politics, should become the art of the impossible, he never lost heart; he never felt sorry for himself; he must have felt exasperated at times, but he never showed resentment. Like Queen Victoria, he was not interested in the possibilities of defeat, except perhaps to circumvent them. He was never a defeatist. If baffled, he was baffled to fight better. When I think of him . . . I am reminded of those lines of Browning:

> One who never turned his back but marched breast
>   forward,
> Never doubted clouds would break,
> Never dreamed, though right were worsted, wrong
>   would triumph,
> Held we fall to rise, are baffled to fight better,
> Sleep to wake.

IV

The selection of the route we wish to make through life, where neither justice nor sin is involved, must always be a decision we have to make for ourselves. We are called to live by faith. We may be privileged to receive dazzling insights given to few. There may be special occasions where our path is lit and our judgement helped, but most of us have no experience of such interventions, and need to muster our own personal resources so that we can muddle through.

Because we are naturally lazy, we tend to rely on those prescriptions which in the past have served us well. Like patent remedies for gout, arthritis, or insomnia, and all our other aches and pains, we all have our pet solutions on which we like to bet because, like a good horse, in the past they have not let us down.

Our own experience may provide us with useful guidelines. The danger is that we try to turn them into lifelines, and fail to realize that in so doing we have now ceased to think, and are in fact becoming imprisoned in an irrelevant world of mottos, clichés and slogans. New problems must be confronted on present evidence, and not on the irrelevant accumulated wisdom of the past. Should I give my child a new toy, my wife a new coat; should we spend more money on our garden, our house, or give it to the starving millions? Like the Chancellor of the Exchequer preparing his budget, we have to balance the imponderables.

On these occasions I find I always meet a man who knows all the answers. Because he is convinced, he thinks he has made up his mind. Because he knows he is a man of Principle and maybe has a Cause he thinks he has a mission to solve all men's problems. On these occasions remember St. Paul's reply, 'I also have the Holy Spirit'. The advice of the man who thinks he is inspired should be treated with reserve and weighed, not necessarily rejected. At least he may unwittingly encourage us to reflect on what we really ought to do.

We have all met too many men whose mothers thought their specially favoured son must have a vocation to the priesthood, or their delightful daughter should be encouraged to marry a suitable young man. The poor boys and girls really had no chance. Others made up their minds for them as to what they should do with their lives. No wonder that later in life the freedom of their choices was sometimes called into question, and priests were freed from their vows and marriages dissolved.

Our choices must be our own. No one can make them for us, nor should we try to choose for others, whether they be husbands or wives, children after they have started to grow up, or the elderly. It is not good for man to be pushed around. We need respect, and freedom too to make our own mistakes.

Most of us have been privileged to know young men and women on fire with the love of Christ, determined to do good in their own particular way. Opposition was seen as a challenge from the devil. Whatever they read, especially in the Bible, confirmed them in their good resolutions. Like most of us, they had mixed motives, but they were generous and wanted to serve. In God's good time their flaws and imperfections will be hammered out on the anvil of life. It is not for us to quench the fire, but to fan it, so that what there is of very human dross and impurity, which would otherwise mar the gifts they offer, may be consumed by their love. What is lost because of love is never felt as loss—nor is it lost—for purified, transformed, it becomes pure gain, and is embodied into our being. That is surely the way by which we and the whole Body of God's people are to be made fit for the Vision of God.

I was very struck some years ago when a South American Bishop pleaded that not only the comity of nations, but the Church, too, should accept this principle. Too often, he said, had the rich, because they were rich, thought they understood the problems of the poor better than the poor themselves. But the rich had no experience of what it felt like to be very poor. Sometimes almost all that is left to the poor is their personal knowledge of their own situation—to deprive them of that, to despise it or ignore it, is to deny them their human dignity. No economic help can compensate for that. We must respect their right not only to live their own lives, but to decide how they should be lived.

Like most of us, I can think of many men I have known who had Principles or adopted Causes. They seemed sometimes to do more harm than good. Not that their causes, like a better distribution of wealth, solving unemployment and inadequate housing, and justice and peace in the world, were not very good. But the do-gooder so often has the knack of making things worse; good-naturedly he interferes in what is not his business, and seeks to impose his vision for mankind. Our good works have to begin at home, and those which events impose on us are far more important than those which we select. We always need to march forward on a road of our own choosing in the direction we think best, but with the humility to alter course as our vision clears and more important issues are revealed.

The man who fell among thieves lay and watched men passing him by, going their way intent on their own vision, their cause, their lawful business, to which they had dedicated their lives. Alas, their cause did not include the unexpected beggar who was an unwanted part of their lives. They did not wish to see him, they had no time for him because they had not put him there and he did not fit in with their ideas. Only the good Samaritan saw God in the present, and was not distracted by his own favourite vision. Too easily we can deceive ourselves.

A cause built on crumpled people who have been passed by is like a life of sin; it carries within it the seeds of its own destruction. We must have causes, but we must beware, for causes are made for man, not man for causes. When causes and ideas take over it is people who suffer. Unless our cause, however good and just and necessary it may appear, is always subordinate to the cause of charity, it will not help our fellow men, and in the last analysis it is only people who matter; whatever else is worthy of our attention, it is charity, the love of our fellow men, which must dominate our choices all through our lives: the means and the end.

8   Confrontations

I

'THERE's a storm brewing'—the words may spell disaster if
we are ill-prepared in an open boat at sea; but those same
words may spell a welcome challenge which we accept with
relish as we button up our collars, pull our caps more firmly
over our ears, lengthen our stride and fill our lungs with fresh
cool country air. If we are ready for the fight why should we
fear? Instinctively we look up and survey the situation. We
may indeed have set off for a country walk half-hoping for,
half-hearing just such a confrontation. A storm for which we
are prepared is an exhilarating experience: we can tense our
muscles and prove our training has been well worth while. As
an opening batsman who has just taken guard looks around him
and inspects the field, so we scan the horizon and note the fast-
changing cloud formation and the darkening skies. We sniff the
air and listen to that eerie silence. Expectancy is everywhere.

That final almost hectic chattering of the birds gradually wanes and dies away, just as in a vast crowded theatre, when the lights are dimmed, a hush descends as though imposed and the chitter-chatter quickly fades. Behind the curtain, the stillness and silence are of a different nature. The actors, there, are alert, and strain with concentration as they think themselves still deeper into the parts they are called upon to play. Their silence is not enforced from outside as if by an irate master imposing silence on a cowed class of little boys, but comes from that self-discipline each one demands from himself. Like cowled monks deep in prayer within their cloister, they harvest their resources. So, too, the silent stillness that bespeaks the imminence of the storm must be discerned. It is not like that passive, tranquil silence of a sweet summer evening when the day's work is done; nor yet is it that deathly stillness of the silent night when the world is deep in sleep, and you can only guess that there is an unheard gentle breathing which will erupt again with noisy life when the dawn breaks. The silence before the storm is of a different species.

It has the awesome quality of a special occasion. As it occurs but rarely, we think of it as in a sense unnatural. The silence threatens, pregnant with suppressed violence. All the forces of nature seem to be gathering their energies for a concerted onslaught. As when the conductor raises his baton and we wait in suspense for the orchestra to respond to his command, so is the lull before the storm. The conductor is hidden, but the harmony and unity of nature are revealed. The silence of the birds, the stillness of the leaves upon the trees, the long grass in the meadows standing motionless, all wait in expectation. Our senses fill the emptiness with meaning. The scentless air, the absent wind, the failing light in unison cry out: 'You have been warned'. We would indeed be foolish if we did not heed the signs.

The wind, the rain, the lightning are but parts of the whole storm. To see things in perspective is never easy, especially when we are distracted from considering the whole by the violence of one part of the attack. We have to summon up our energies to stand firm. In our desire to escape the drenching rain we may forget for a moment the violence of the wind, and then caps and buttons fly and an umbrella is speedily destroyed. We try to get back our breath and shelter from the wind beneath a tree, and forget that lightning and falling branches may bring much worse disaster. When we are violently attacked by the forces of nature in a storm at sea or on an unknown mountainside, we need to remain cool and keep our heads. But when the attack comes from our fellow men, then the onslaught is psychologically more difficult to withstand, and a balanced judgement and a discerning eye are vitally important. We need to learn to read the warning signs, to take some elementary precautions, to see things in perspective as parts of a greater whole. In the ballet and in the bull-fight, and even on the cricket-field, the silent stillness speaks of a hidden power which will erupt and suddenly flash forth. To survive that potentially destructive moment, to harness that superabundant energy and conduct it into safer channels, where it can make a positive contribution to the good of men, should be the object of all our confrontations.

It is not easy to harness what is wild. The stories of the Mid-West a hundred years ago and the rearing bucking bronchos spring to mind. Unharnessed wild horses which no man could ride were like that storm at sea—magnificent to behold, and full of danger too; but they were of little use to man unless they could be withstood and possibly controlled. To foresee and survive a violent storm, to conquer and control wild horses, calls for skills, courage, and self-discipline, as well as a cool head. Such qualities will be essential if we are to withstand and harness those outbursts of human psychic energy which cause most human confrontations. That is a task we should not shun. Although we know from our limited experience that many confrontations do more harm than good, and we are sometimes better off without them, they can be necessary. To try to avoid them may be to court disaster for ourselves and those who are dear to us. We need to be prepared.

Many people doing their first or second job in an office or

factory or shop are totally unprepared. Unexpectedly they find themselves under attack from those who do not share their moral values. They find their views on justice and sex are called into question before they have been fully formulated. They are told they are being cut down to size, as though they were necessarily big-headed because they have viewpoints of their own. It is often their Christian standards which provoke the attack. For it is a curious fact that the so-called permissive society does not so easily tolerate those who have an ethical code which is different from its own.

'Why', they are asked, 'does your Church forbid abortion?' and the implication is that the Church is cruel and the questioner more kind. 'Why is your Church so old-fashioned on premarital sex and sex in general, and on euthanasia?' and the conclusion is that the Church is out of date and therefore no longer relevant for modern man. The questions can go on for ever. The fighting in Ireland and South America are grist to the mill. All through the barrage of attack the theme song is usually the same: you are not free, you have not grown up, you are still brain-washed by priests and nuns and that vague thing called the Church.

In their perplexity no wonder many young and innocent people are made miserable; they experience a sense of guilt; they search for solutions and feel inadequate to answer all the charges so freely laid upon their doorstep. What should they do, what should they say?

The answer is very simple; they must attack. Instead of trying to answer the question, they need first to find out why the questions are being asked. Is their questioner merely an attacker, or is he interested in knowing the answer? If, as is often the case, it is a predatory male who wants the girl to sleep with him, or someone whose sole concern is that everyone should support the malpractices he proposes, then a simple answer is irrelevant. The attacker is concerned with action, and the only remedy is to expose him with a further question.

'Why do you want to know?' 'Would you be interested in becoming a Christian if I tell you?' 'Why not?' 'Do you accept the authority of God or God's Commandments, or maybe Christ or maybe the Church?'—'and if not, why not?'

Only by such ripostes are the real questions which lay behind the original questionings unmasked. This may look like mental gymnastics, winning a verbal argument, but usually it is more than that. If the questions were sincere, no harm is done. But if their motives were less honest, and the aim was to humiliate and undermine, then once the attack has been exposed for the cowardly thing it was, the questioner will probably lose his temper; he will not like being challenged. Peace can now return to the office and, if anyone is going to hand in his resignation, it will not be the girl whose life was being made a misery, but the immediate boss or fellow-worker who was trying to take it out of her. Sometimes to attack, to ask the questions, is the kindest thing to do.

II

However, it would be a mistake to think that all confrontations are the result of sin. The three days' loss and the finding of the Child Jesus in the Temple in Jerusalem, as narrated by St. Luke, is a good example to the contrary. There was no question of sin, but Our Lady was bewildered and could not understand what was happening. Our Lord was equally surprised: 'Did you not know that I must be about my Father's business?' Their intimate personal relationship suffered a sudden shock. The tension had arisen because Christ was growing into manhood, with all the new social responsibilities which that involved. As he acquired a new status within society, the pattern which had governed the former mother–child relationship was modified. All growth involves tension, a stretching forth like the roots of the plant groping into deeper soil in search of food, confronting the unknown and unknowable, which may be friendly, able to be assimilated, or hostile, deadly to the touch. No wonder fear is not far away. Each new growth puts stresses and strains on all the other relationships which are the main constituents of our being as human persons and, unless those relationships are vital and alive, they will snap like the rope of the net which has become brittle through drying for too long in the sun. The mother–child relationship needed to mature to that deeper understanding which can unite two adults. The old remained, but a new, even more wonderful relationship emerged as a result of that creative tension.

Many confrontations are less creative than that described by St. Luke, and some confrontations are trivial. No one much minds disagreements with someone they do not know: a stranger jumping the bus queue in the street, a lorry-driver overtired and exasperated after a long day at the wheel. One can find oneself caught up in a situation certainly not of one's own choosing, and faced with a confrontation which has been sparked off by a whole series of incidents, like a family row when one trips over the cat, upsets milk over the new tablecloth and impatiently lets everyone have a piece of one's mind. That is an aspect of life with which we are all only too familiar, and usually, unless we are caught off our guard, or well below our normal form, it is the sort of confrontation we can defuse and soon laugh about. It may damage our pride, and tell us something about ourselves which we do not want to know. On balance, it probably does us more good than harm in that it increases our self-knowledge.

St. Teresa of Avila used to say that virtue is only established as a virtue after it has been tried. So often we assume that we have spiritual muscle, but confrontations show us our mistake, and what we took for virtue we find is really the absence of temptation. We should pray: Lord, lead us not into temptations with which we cannot cope. There are some confrontations we need to be spared, but some we must learn to face with courage.

III

Everyone with responsibility for others knows the sinking

feeling that comes when he realizes that confrontations are called for with those he loves. The timing does not always rest with us. Most husbands and wives, mothers and fathers are faced with such necessary confrontations from time to time. I recall the memory of a tall priest, over six feet, who had his own special way of solving marital disagreements. As soon as he suspected that all was not well in the home, he would call and ask the husband and wife to kneel on the carpet before the fireplace in what they called the 'front room'. Then he would stand over them and proceed to remind them of their duties and responsibilities towards each other and their children, and even the Church, if they were failing in that too. The poor couple could only fix their eyes on his enormous shoes or on the baggy trousers out of shape at the knees which were at the same level as their eyes. Whilst the good Father went on and on they stayed on their knees, and sometimes, with an effort, craned their necks to try to look up at the stern forbidding face of the man who was haranguing them. Usually this effort was too much. With relief the couple would join hands and give each other mutual support until the ordeal was over. Life together may have had its problems, but a visitation from such a priest was infinitely worse, and marital disagreements were seldom heard of in that parish. Couples threatened by such visitations learnt the value of mutual trust and openness with each other. That priest was unusual, and I for one never tried to imitate his tactics.

I remember going to see one man week after week trying to persuade him to return to his responsibilities. It was all in vain. One day, I asked him bluntly, when I had got to know him well, 'Why won't you return to your duties?' His reply was so simple it still amazes me. 'No one has told me to,' he said; he was waiting for an order. All my sweet reasonings and arguments had been wasted. He just wanted to be told. I told him. He obeyed. Life was sometimes, though I found it and still find it difficult to believe, as simple as that. Often that is all we need from one another. Confrontations are sometimes quite unnecessary, especially with children; sometimes too they can be dissolved by laughter. One man I knew was amused by difficulties, and his attitude made most of them more bearable. His mere presence tended to dissipate the disparate forces that were building up into a storm, so that the need for confrontations seldom arose.

However, most mothers and fathers are often faced with difficult confrontations with their children when they seek to bring discipline into their lives. They may be only over minor points like cleaning out the bath after they have used it, sharing their toys with others, helping with the washing up, or putting tools back in their proper place; they may be about more serious matters such as not treating their home like a hostel, taking everything their parents do for them for granted, or not wanting to go to church or to a Catholic school. It is of course within the home that a right attitude to these necessary confrontations, which we all need for our growth towards maturity, should be learnt. If the right attitude is not learnt when we are very young we may find, in later life, that minor but necessary confrontations produce damaging after-effects.

Every relationship needs to be tested. As the leafy foliage of the English oak tree flutters in the gentlest of breezes, the tree retains an inner rigidity and capacity for growth. It bends before the wind and sheds its leaves when shaken, yet remains unmoved, and sends forth new shoots and new buds in its own time. Relationships can be strengthened, personalities developed, and deeper roots established by tensions. Dislike them though we may, they should enrich us every time.

Confrontations are necessary too for the deepening of those friendships which we need throughout our life. When Cardinal Allen left Oxford in Elizabethan times to found the English College at Douai for the training of young priests, he insisted they should try to keep up their friendships with those they had left behind in England. One of the men who benefited whilst still teaching at Oxford was St. Edmund Campion. He too learnt the lesson when he went to Douai. Allen knew that such correspondence would be full of heartaches and wear and tear on the emotions, but judged such confrontations should be encouraged. When I see his statue in his old College, Oriel, overlooking St. Mary's and the High, I often think how right and courageous he was.

It is our mental attitude to confrontations which is all-important. Like surgery, it should not be indulged in except when necessary, but when it is necessary delay is mutually harmful. I suspect the clergy, out of a sense of mistaken kindness, have too often procrastinated when action was called for.

The main confrontations with which the clergy used to be faced between themselves tended to be concerned with women or drink. Both are matters on which celibate priests are inclined to be sensitive, and often, especially in the case of drink, confrontations were postponed. In recent years such delays have been recognized to be disastrous. Once alcoholism became acknowledged as a disease, and not a moral fault, treatment was easily provided. But the problem had to be confronted. The question of women friends was even more delicate, but here too one would think a greater spirit of mutual trust has made confrontations between priests and their superiors easier than it used to be.

Today the confrontations that take place between the clergy are more likely to be over their respective attitudes to changes in the Church. Some tend to look back with nostalgia to simpler days when issues were more sharply defined; others tend to be so concerned with the needs of people that they are impatient with rules and laws. All will try to face up to what the Gospels tell us is the message of Christ, and will hope to put their trust in prayer and the Holy Spirit; but we will have to go on learning all our lives, and many confrontations may be necessary to shake us out of our hard-line simplistic misunderstanding of the Church and the needs of the world around us.

There are other confrontations which must take place within the boardroom no less than in the home or presbytery. It used to be said that the American businessman was better about this than the Englishman. The Americans were concerned about the good of the firm; the English were more concerned about having to live together subsequently within a sort of club. The Americans were to that extent more objective, and could disagree without becoming personally involved; the English found this more difficult. I would not be sure how valid the distinction is, but fear of confrontation may easily lead one to shelve a problem, and hope it will go away. Delaying tactics seldom solve the problem.

Admittedly, if one delays in writing letters they may eventually no longer need answering. There is the story of Don Vasco de Quiroga, a brilliant Spanish lawyer who met St. Thomas More in Flanders when the two men were engaged in diplomatic missions there. Don Vasco was greatly impressed by the economic and sociological ideas developed in More's book *Utopia*, and when several years later he became governor of the state of Michoacán, in Mexico, he decided to implement many of its suggestions. The result was an outstanding improvement in the welfare and prosperity of the people; and eventually Don Vasco wrote to St. Thomas More to thank him for his inspiration. The letter arrived three weeks after St. Thomas had lost his head. Whilst time solves all problems, there are some which demand other solutions.

IV

It is important to realize that not only our heads but also our hearts our involved in confrontations. If it were only a question of heads, then a computer could solve our problems for us. If it were only our hearts, then it would merely be a question of tastes and preferences, like preferring one school of architecture or one school of painting to another. We can live in peace with a man who prefers Beethoven to Brahms, provided he does not play it too loud, or with a man whose colour schemes revolt us. We can compromise on questions of taste without feeling we are personally under attack. We can agree to differ.

But when the confrontations strike deeper into our heads as well as our hearts, when it becomes a question of ideals and ideologies, then we are in deeper water. Whenever a man says to me 'this is a matter of principle', I can sense the storm-clouds gathering. Today there is little real dispute about means; in this technological world the adaptations of means to ends changes every day—we are happy to learn, and content to admit our ignorance on new techniques.

I remember a religious telling me that when working on a parish he had a motor bicycle which had an electric as well as a kick starter. Naturally enough he was using the electric starter when his superior happened to pass by, and explained that he should use the kick starter, as this would be better for the machine. He obeyed. Some years later he moved to another parish, and again found himself in a similar situation, with another motor bicycle which also had a kick as well as an electric starter. He proceeded to use the kick starter, as his former superior had advised. On this occasion his new superior passed by, and told him he should not use the kick but the electric starter, as this would save the machine. Life it seems to me is largely composed of trivia at which we can afford to laugh. We all love to pontificate and exercise an authority we often do not have, and few of us are experts in more than one very limited and restricted field. Such confrontations as arise on the right adaptations of means to ends can usually be solved, if we so choose, by consulting the appropriate reference books.

But in disagreements about the end, the final objective, there we find that confrontations take on a bitterness which seems to reveal a deep-rooted pride, or is it prejudice, or arrogance—or just fear? It all goes under the name of principle—but of course both sides have principles and claim to be fighting for Truth, Justice, and Charity; and that is what makes it so difficult when neither side can see how they can abandon their position.

There was a day not long ago when heresy was considered the greatest evil, to be avoided at all costs. The Anti-Modernist

Oath with all its formality and endless anathemas, must have made a lasting impression on young men going on for the priesthood. The very form of the teaching methods in seminaries, with the emphasis on the thesis as the statement about the truth which ought to be held and the concomitant list of adversaries who had to be combated, produced a mentality where the truth could be neatly parcelled up, known, and adhered to, and the positions of the adversaries had to be avoided.

The more positive approach which seems to be pursued today makes the search for truth exciting and honest. Not that the old ways were dishonest, but they presumed a mentality which would accept the situation as it had been hammered out over the centuries, whereas the more modern way leaves much more room for the creative contributions of the young. We need all the insights we can get, so we should I think be grateful for the new ways. Even though some of the clarity which used to delight us has gone, so too have the over-rigid interpretations of the legalistic mind. The concept of the pilgrim church prepares us to face the challenge of the future, and encourages us to cling to our identity, but not the trappings of the past. Not surprisingly, there are still difficulties in which we find our heads as well as our hearts involved.

Though confrontations are disagreeable to the old, to my surprise I suddenly realized that they present no such problems to the young. Why should they? The young have been trained to search for the truth; they have had to face confrontations all through their studies—and have learnt to enjoy trying to justify the positions they have taken up. They are not afraid to disagree, and indeed enjoy it, though I do not think it would be fair to say that they are playing intellectual games, or are guilty of the sin of philosophical contraception, to which many intellectuals are tempted—i.e. enjoying the legitimate pleasure of intellectual inquiry, but reluctant to be burdened with the end-product which entails commitment to an established position. They are not just out for the hunt, with no fox in view. No, they are as deadly serious as were the older generation, but they are well used to confrontations, and have learnt to live with them.

They can easily disagree with a young priest leaving the priesthood, and yet enter into close personal relationships with him and his new wife in a way which would still be embarrassing to an older generation. Confrontations in private or in public, in the press or in open debate, on the platform or on the television, are all seen as perfectly acceptable. Such confrontations, which to an older generation looked like letting down the side in public, and were in bad taste, are seen by the young as thoroughly good. They are open-minded, and do not want to paper over the cracks. They try to be completely honest, and would urge those who disagree with them to have the courage and honesty to say so openly. They see things in black and white, but accept realistically, or try to, that we have to live in a grey world of compromise.

In the long run the blood pressure will benefit. Life may not be so comfortable but, as we are constantly reminded, even St. Peter and St. Paul thought it necessary to disagree in public, and not over non-essentials.

V

But when confrontations are inevitable and necessary, there are some rules we should remember. Charity must remain paramount. This means that we must be concerned with the good of those with whom we are in conflict. If the discussion gets off on the wrong foot, which it can so easily do, by implying fault, then all is quickly lost, and a row develops which leaves only bitterness behind, and nothing is achieved. If we can identify ourselves with those with whom we are in confrontation, so that together we tackle a common problem, then the difficulties sink into the background as we unite against a common foe. The 'we' slipped in can win an ally, where the 'you' implies complaint, guilt, slackness, or some other heinous crime. 'We ought to do something about . . .' as against 'You ought to do something about . . .' creates a very different picture; the one appeals to all the higher instincts, the other puts us on our self-defence, and then indeed we can expect a few broadsides ourselves for which we may be utterly unprepared.

The old Chinese insistence about never losing face seems to me as important in the West as ever it was in the East. No one likes to be criticized; the juster the criticism, the more difficult it is to bear, and the deeper the resentment. If the criticism is not true why should we worry? But if the criticism is justified and hits the nail on the head, then indeed it may be difficult for us not to feel humiliated, and to retain or re-establish the former good relations.

It was said of one of the old monks in the desert, Arsenius by name, that he used to cross his knees at recreation in the evening. This was considered by the rest of the community to be disedifying, especially on the part of such an otherwise saintly old man. So the rest of the monks agreed that the next day one of the younger monks should cross his knees and that then the Prior should notice it and rebuke him. When this happened the young man uncrossed his legs with shame and confusion. No one let it appear they had noticed the old Arsenius quietly uncrossing his legs. So was correction given without loss of face, without unnecessary shame, or confrontation for such a minor matter. The story is probably apocryphal, but has a message even for today.

With a little thought some confrontations can often be avoided and the desired end achieved. To bring people back to their responsibilities it is more effective to get them to help someone else who is in even greater need, and in the course of helping others they often manage to sort out their own problems. Time and again an older brother will put his own house in order so that he can help a younger brother or sister whom he loves. Like most of us, he is willing to do for others what he cannot be bothered to do for himself.

This was one of the lessons which St. Ignatius was always

anxious to implant; a truth discovered for ourselves is worth far more than one which we are told. But there is no reason why we should not try to set the scenario, when it lies in our power, so that others may have an opportunity to learn. I wonder sometimes if many a boy or girl has not gained a fuller grasp of the deeper truths of life through acting in a play than they would ever have had they merely been taught them in the class-room.

When talking about confrontations there is another danger which I think we should avoid. Some think that openness will solve all problems; that if only people are fully open to each other, they will be helped to be fully open to themselves, and then they will be genuine, fully integrated persons. Clearly there is a much-needed truth in this assertion, but I think there is a fallacy too. Our Lord only slowly revealed the truth to his Apostles. He never tried to finish the task. He left this to the Holy Spirit, and over the centuries the Church has been growing in her understanding of the truth, and presumably will continue to do this for all time. The truth can never be exhausted, nor can the potential of the individual. If we are right in thinking that man was made to the image and likeness of God, then there is something infinite in man, and this can never be fully known.

So, too, on another and different level, it may be dangerous and wrong to try to tell a man the truth about himself. He may not be able to take it at the present moment. The more certain you are that what you want to tell him is the truth, the more important it may be not to tell him all of it just now. There are many things we need to learn in the fullness of time, when we are capable of coping with the situation; to learn before we are ready may break us. I have known several men over the years who have been subjected to some form or other of group dynamics and who, whilst at first euphoric about their experiences, in the long run appear to have had major breakdowns when they found that the rarefied atmosphere they had breathed when all were enjoying equal openness of spirit did not continue on into the toil and moil of the religious life and the class-room. That was many years ago, today the techniques may have improved. But I suspect it still remains true that most of us may be more damaged than helped by revelations about ourselves before the ground has been prepared and we are ready to accept the reality as it really is. Much will depend on the nature of the interpersonal relationships. I remember two great friends who had known each other well for over thirty years having a violent disagreement. They knew each other so well, and were tied together by so many strands of friendship, that they could afford to quarrel, and even question and finally break one or two strands of their relationship, knowing that the other strands would stand the strain. In the same way a parent and an erring son, a husband and wife, a religious superior and his subjects should be so bound together by mutual trust that they can afford to differ on many smaller points. They may have the responsibility of telling each other some of the home truths that we all need to learn, but only so much as is necessary, only when the time is ripe, only under a very clear umbrella of charity and love. The timing and the occasion and the overall atmosphere are all-important.

There may of course be other occasions when the good of a third party demands the truth be told, and told now, but even then it is necessary that the utmost care be taken in the telling. There are ways and ways of telling, and unless there is a clear and manifest love and goodwill between the persons the result may be disastrous.

There are disagreements which need to be brought up to the boil before the poisons can be rendered innocuous. How many marriages have broken down because neither party had the courage to confront the other on the basic issues on which they were divided; ultimately all lines of communication between them silted up, and they could only talk about safe subjects, the trivia of life, and became ever more isolated and lonely in their own lives.

VI

Would it be fair to say that sometimes confrontations are a blessing from God? They lead us on out of the accustomed places we know and love so well, and where we love to vegetate, to new places and new pursuits apparently less attractive, but with a freshness all their own. New challenges, confrontations and calls for adaptations may lead us to modify so many of those prejudices we have loved for a long lifetime, and although we may have a sense of loss when we let them go or have to modify them, who can deny that in the long run our lives may be enormously enriched? When the wild storm is over we are like new-born men: re-tooled, re-tuned, purged and purified, our lives like an old pencil re-sharpened to a point it had long since lost. We feel we have grown in stature, and there is a new spring in our step.

The greater our authority, the more responsible our position, whether in the family, the school, or the community, the more important will be the virtue of prudence. Whilst the good sneeze clears the head, and a flaming row, like a thunderstorm, may sometimes be necessary and the only way to clear the air—we have the example of St. John the Baptist dealing with the Pharisees and Our Lord driving the buyers and sellers out of the Temple to encourage us in this—for the most part we have to be careful not to upset or scandalize others, especially by voicing our own personal views as those of the Church. The good artist, we are told, should jolt people out of their comfortable preconceptions as to what is beautiful, and so enable them to see things freshly as they really are. He gives them the chance to have a new vision, or perhaps it would be more realistic to say he helps them to remove those dark glasses which they have worn since birth, which hide and distort much of the world around them. Today, when theological and social and moral preconceptions are so confused, confrontations would seem to be inevitable and necessary; but so too is the virtue of prudence, and this is perhaps the virtue that has been lacking.

St. Thomas More is the example of the man we need today—strong in his own personal convictions, but very chary of imposing his views on others.

9   Sharing

In Wales there is a ten-mile stretch of road, from Dolgellau to Barmouth, which has some of the most beautiful views to be seen in the British Isles. On the northern side, the mountains rise so steeply that their summits cannot be seen from the road which runs along the side of the estuary to the sea. Cader Idris, with Penmaen Pool nestling at its foot, dominates the view to the south, and is mirrored in the still water of the estuary when the tide is in.

The road, carried along the narrow man-made shelf close to the water's edge, twists like a snake. Each corner, so typical of Wales, reveals new and unexpected views, with the old railway bridge across the mouth of the estuary providing a permanent frame, an unchanging contrast, a sombre sight illustrating man's achievement set against the glory of the woods, the mountains, and the sea.

We used to travel the road frequently, and it was the ever-changing colours of the estuary which first caught our attention. In the summer the brilliant blues of the shallow water would change in a few seconds to emerald green, reflecting the wooded hillsides. In the autumn the purple tints and bracken gave it a different hue. As the tide ebbed glistening yellow sands stretched to the bridge, beyond which lay the sea.

Sometimes the hills and estuary are momentarily lost to sight as the road tunnels through the solid rock of the over-hanging cliffs, or winds beneath arched trees which used to meet, before the road was widened, like the vaulting of a cathedral nave high overhead. Near the coast in Wales, the light filters through the trees with a quality all its own. In spring and autumn it has a clarity, a dazzling element like diamonds, but with soft overtones enticing, bewitching, haunting, fleeting, which has to be seen to be believed. From the road as you suddenly emerge from comparative darkness into dazzling light, it is as though you were behind a powerful spotlight filtering the rays of the sun and the reflections from the water, and directing your attention now this way, now that. The hills and the wide expanse of the estuary seem alive as the shadows of the clouds add the poetry of movement to what had never for a moment been a static scene.

Some of us at such moments like to be alone with nature, to be free to savour all that we can see and smell, to explore and indulge our childish fancies as we pause or follow tracks we have never passed before. In such a place, in such a mood, we are self-sufficient as we puff out our chests and fill our lungs with pure air, and sit or stand in peace while the landscape dances from one mood to another before our eyes.

Sometimes we need to share our excitement, and find our perception and enjoyment are disproportionately increased as we seek to explain what gives us so much delight. The artist, the poet, and the musician are enormously enriched in their own personal appreciation through their efforts, however inadequate artistically, to preserve their vision which, like a startled hare or a fish rising in a pool as the evening falls, vanishes as soon as it is seen. A vision shared proves richer and more lasting than one we keep to ourselves. We may be conscious that our efforts are in vain. We know that, despite all we may do to preserve what we so much enjoy, much of the magic inevitably eludes us and seeps away. But that which is shared takes on a lasting quality.

Before the war it was often said that 'there is no impression without expression'. Only what we seek to express, whatever the medium we choose, becomes inalienably our own. What we fail to give to others, so that they may share it with us, proves ephemeral and does not stand the test of time. Only by transposing what we treasure in our hearts to words, or paint, or music, or pieces of old rock or stone which we would sculpt, does the hidden, incomprehensible, and inexpressible vision get digested and becomes our own.

This old truth we all know well, and it has many applications, as everyone who has ever tried to teach can easily appreciate. Often a parent or a priest is far from being a qualified teacher, and the recipient of his kindly-meant ministrations does not become much wiser because of his inarticulate efforts. But the parents always find themselves enriched by their efforts, and the poor priest who struggles to explain mysterious Old Testament passages so as to help his congregation enter more fully into the life of God never struggles in vain. Each member of his congregation may well remain bewildered by the curious passages selected to help him live as an *alter Christus* in the modern world, but those who seek to teach always find their own insights and appreciation enhanced.

For most of us who teach in these situations there are no final answers, only a greater approximation to the truth. But as a result of our efforts we take another step or two along the road of life, we pass another corner and find ourselves faced with a new solution; and, we can hope, we have also helped those we've sought to teach.

Before and shortly after the war I remember many boys at Stonyhurst and at St. Michael's, Leeds, who had the courage of their convictions and were willing to stand up week after week in a variety of places on Catholic Evidence Guild platforms and try to explain their faith. I cannot judge how far their efforts helped to change the face of Britain, but they certainly changed the lives of the speakers. In later life a very high proportion of those who had so sought to express their faith found their own personal convictions deepened, and became zealous priests.

St. Peter exhorts us to be ready and willing to give a reason for our faith, not just the objective ones which anyone can read up for himself if he so wishes in many excellent manuals, but the subjective reasonings of our own heart. To express our own lived-through experiences in ways helpful to others is never easy. Quite apart from intellectual conviction, it pre-supposes a sensitivity to others' needs and weaknesses as well as to the hidden and mysterious motivations of our own heart which is seldom found.

All of us have met good evangelicals, ebullient charismatics and kindly enthusiasts convinced that their faith can provide a solution for all the problems of a sick, selfish, materialistic, and saddened society. Probably most of their insights, if not all, reflect the wisdom of God. But unless such men have learnt to share their vision with others, they will probably find that they are like hermits in the desert declaiming the mysteries of God to the lonely waste lands, with no one willing to listen to their words.

So often the man who buttonholes one in a public place and exclaims with a glint in his eye that he has something he wants to share is a lecturer *manqué* who needs an audience. Perhaps unintentionally he confers a compliment upon us, as he clearly thinks we shall prove a receptive and captive listener, but sharing is hardly the right word to describe the lecture which ensues.

Too often do we meet such men, thwarted and unable to find the recognition which they think is their due, embittered and increasingly harsh because their message has fallen on deaf ears. They preach long sermons about the need to listen. Perhaps sometimes their own hearts have grown insensitive to the needs of ordinary busy and worried people struggling in that overgrown jungle with the sun lost to sight which we call the world. I suspect that in recent years we have suffered from over-exposure to prophets who have sought to endow their personal traumas with significance for the Church and society. Their efforts have, I think, sometimes been counter-productive, and have put off, rather than attracted, those who tried to listen, although clearly they had a right, perhaps even a duty, so to speak.

More often, so it seems to me, we meet people who are the opposite of vociferous about their faith. Like the good mother, the dedicated social worker, or the sensitive employer, they are only too well aware of the trials and tribulations as they affect most people in the world today, and with their innate respect for the privacy of others they refrain from promulgating their own personal beliefs, visions, and way of life. Their restraint does not arise from a lack of conviction, but from their sensitivity, and from an unwillingness to obtrude their own personal convictions on others unless they are convinced that the time is ripe.

This is an area where most of us all through our lives will have had to do much heart-searching. Should I have spoken up—does standing up and being counted invariably do more good than harm? Should I have openly condemned a course of which I disapproved, and which I was personally convinced would end in disaster, or would I, by terminating a relationship, have done more harm than good? How do I avoid condoning a policy, attitude or act of which I disapprove? The timing is all-important, and I alone can judge.

The moral principles are clear enough. Charity, the good of others, must be paramount. Truth, justice, respect for the rights of others, must also enjoy a sovereign state. But the application of principles calls for insights into imponderables which inevitably elude us. How will those we wish to help react if and when we tell them the truth as we, in our own hearts, know it is? Are we interfering in matters which are not our concern, and where others, with better insights than our own, already have the business well in hand?

There is a time for sharing, and there is a time too for standing alone, upright, buffeted by the winds and sea. Those who rely solely on their personal example are traditionally depicted as a beacon or a lighthouse on a headland warning those in danger of shipwreck at sea; perhaps traffic lights at a notoriously dangerous intersection or crossroads would have a more obvious meaning for most people today. We alone can make that decision as to whether we should be sharing our insights or standing alone, signalling red or green, or resorting to a cowardly 'Out of Order' notice and condoning what we cannot justify.

The difficulty of making such a decision as to whether we should speak of those deep and sacred things which we treasure in our hearts, or whether we should remain silent and rely on the witness of our lives to help those who are in deep distress, is enormously complicated today by much unhelpful advice to which we are all subjected from the mass media. Respect for the judgement, integrity, and intelligence of the listener and viewer would seem to be low on the list of priorities which motivate those responsible for providing us with information or entertainment. The morality of advertising calls for more expert treatment than I can provide, but those of us who are inevitably subjected to the influence of the mass media are unlikely to find it has made us more sensitive to the silent, unvoiced aspirations of our fellow man. More likely, our reaction will be to join in—for that is after all the objective which the media seek to provoke, and they are not unskilled—and, in the name of common sense, to try to secure a hearing for our own viewpoint. It may well be that we shall be surprised to recognize that shrill voice as our own as we seek to make ourselves heard above the din.

We may, of course, react with Anglo-Saxon stoic patience, and purse our lips as we keep our own counsels firmly locked away as our personal and private business, rather like those stern, admirable, and unattractive governesses we read of in our youth, who had a Jeeves-like quality which was not easily drawn. Imperious they may sometimes have been, but few could dispute their basic loyalty and common sense.

But the dilemma persists. Of course a roman collar, or a

brood of unruly small children who are obviously one's own, introduces an extra element, like secretly putting gin into the glass of an unsuspecting friend, and can usually be guaranteed to set off a chain reaction amongst quite ordinary people which may bewilder the casual onlooker. The young cleric or religious who openly admits he is trying to serve God will find himself treated with confidences from comparative strangers, who are glad to have an opportunity to share some of their own half-formulated hopes and fears with another who, by his way of life, has demonstrated his interest in their particular terrain. Those whom we meet casually on wild and inaccessible tracks in the mountains of Wales can usually be relied on to share some of our basic values and philosophy of life; so, too, a mother will seek out another, and those hoping for greater understanding of spiritual values are naturally drawn to confide in those who publicly proclaim their concern about and their commitment to the propagation of such values. We can easily share with those whose lives bear witness to their sympathy with our own ideals, not in a teacher–taught relationship, but as between equals concerned in scaling new and unexplored heights.

For the young cleric this is a relationship he often has difficulty in establishing. He finds himself looked on as a spiritual guru, an expert guide who already knows the secrets of the mountain wastes. Whilst he is hoping for a friend with whom to share his exhilaration, he finds instead a pupil expecting to be taught. 'Am I not a mere man, too?' he cries, as he pulls off his dog-collar and gets into his polo-neck sweater. His understandable reaction is not always helpful. Worthwhile relationships are neither made nor marred by such trivia as dress, and whilst a roman collar may sometimes be useful in the initial stages in helping a stranger to find a sympathetic ear, it can be harmful when it would encourage either friend or priest to dress up this relationship.

It is our basic humanity and our common ignorance and sense of striving to attain what we have only dimly glimpsed which enables us to share anything worth while. Our paper qualifications and our dreary degrees and expertise are only too often irrelevant, and can be stumbling-blocks rather than aids. We have all met young men in their early thirties who have settled into a way of life as perpetual students—their pockets bulge with degrees and credits gained as a result of remarkable assiduity. So often they have also acquired a chip on their shoulder. No one wants to buy their expertise. Computers with ready-made answers and those who have solutions to all the world's problems are no adequate substitute for lesser human beings who are willing to share our wonder, awe, and enchantment at the views and visions suddenly provided at each twist and turn as our road snakes through life. The grandeur of God may always dominate our landscape, but there is so much more to be seen which also reflects his presence which we can more easily grasp and usefully share with our fellow men.

Some people, we may consider, can be relied upon to provide us with a sympathetic ear because we know that they themselves have come through some dreadful experience, or because of a special position they hold, or because of something they have done. Most converts fall into this last category, and they can expect, as an opening gambit across the dinner-table or a gin and it, or even across a cup of tea, a kindly (and sometimes not so kindly) inquiry as to why they have changed, or adopted a new faith. Some inquirers are frankly puzzled that anyone should seek to get out of, or into, the established order. They realize, at least in their subconscious, that this is a momentous decision, and they clearly wonder how anyone can have the temerity to make it. Behind their genuine, puzzled, question lies the implication: 'Who do you think you are, you must have an exaggerated sense of your own importance so to tamper with the existing order which is good enough for your peers, who are far more intelligent than you are, and better persons to boot.' We have all heard the unspoken criticism pouring out behind the puffing of a pipe or over the rattling of a genteel cup of tea. Sometimes admiration for anyone who is prepared single-handed to take on the

Establishment seeps through, but more often hostility lies not far behind the question, and can be easily detected. Too often, I suspect, the questioner sees an implied criticism of himself in the heroic actions of such converts, and as a result is both resentful and afraid. He is far from being temperamentally prepared for any ripostes which the convert may wish to make as a result of his inquiries.

Yet it would not seem unreasonable if the convert were indeed to enter into the spirit of question and answer to which he has been subjected, and open his own attack. Not too unreasonably he may ask: 'Why have you stayed in the faith of your fathers all your life? Why have you not also changed? Are you convinced and satisfied, or just uninterested—but if the latter, why do you ask me?' Yet the convert who does this will quickly find himself accused of spiritual pride and arrogance, as if, after putting his own house in order, he now takes delight in upsetting others. There are clearly two standards at work, and it is important not to get the wires crossed, or we may have a minor explosion.

The convention would seem to be that the convert has done something in the public forum, and is liable to be questioned as to why he has so acted. On the other hand, the man who has remained unmoved in the situation in which he was born and bred is not expected to justify his stability or perhaps slothfulness, and any questions asked of him are regarded as an impertinence, an undue and unacceptable probing into private affairs which are not our concern.

I remember one lady who, when asked at dinner why she had become a Catholic, rejoined that it was because she thought it was true, and then proceeded to ask the elderly gentleman who was sitting next to her why he had always remained in the faith in which he had been brought up. Her question was considered to be in bad taste, but I wonder if it was. As members of the human race, and still more as members of any given society, we should not be ashamed or afraid to give reasons for our faith. The reasons which we may give may well not be so strictly logical and objectively satisfactory as to stand up to a sustained attack from theological experts, but why should they be? The fact that the reasons which we give only scrape the surface should not surprise us. We all know from experience that our most serious decisions are seldom taken solely as the result of a piece of logical reasoning. As Newman was fond of pointing out in another context, we tend to reach our certitudes as a result of perceiving a whole series of converging probabilities, which can only be explained if the central truth is there—even if that central truth is itself invisible and in another dimension, and incapable of logical proof. I think we all know from experience that the reasons we give, under the pressure of hostile questioning, as to why we acted in a particular way may well be true, but are nearly always inadequate. The totality of the motives which prompt us at any given time nearly always eludes us, and can only be grasped subsequently with the passage of time—if then. This does not mean that we behave irrationally, but that the motivation which inspires us is deeper and wider than our reason.

Just as when we are faced with one of those magnificent panoramic views in the mountains, it is the total experience which causes us to cry out in wonder, and not just the majesty of the mountains, the lakes glistening in the sunshine, or the charm of a near-by bubbling brook. We cannot point to just one thing, for it is the whole experience which moves us. So too when we are asked to explain our motives. Often the most basic and fundamental lie in our subconscious, rooted in our family upbringing, training, and the prejudices of a lifetime which we cannot perceive.

As Christians, of course, there is a further factor which has to be considered before we can explain our actions. For we would all believe that the Holy Spirit should be expected to play a large part in our decision-making, but only with time will this become apparent—if it ever does. Certainly we cannot be expected to summon him as one of the witnesses to the reasonableness of our actions, and yet we believe that without his influence our judgements would certainly be the poorer.

There is a well-known passage in St. Peter's Second Letter which may help to illustrate this truth:

So we have confirmation of what was said in prophecies; and you will be right to depend on prophecy and take it as a lamp for lighting a way through the dark until the dawn comes and the morning star rises in your minds. At the same time, we must be most careful to remember that the interpretation of scriptural prophecy is never a matter for the individual. Why? Because no prophecy ever came from man's initiative. When men spoke for God it was the Holy Spirit that moved them.

All men of good faith will experience this problem from time to time when they are asked to give reasons for their actions and their beliefs, which are seen to be contrary to those adopted by a permissive society, but it is converts or those who have made a more public stand who inevitably will have to bear the brunt of such attacks.

How far we should welcome such inquiries and be prepared to bare our soul in public is a further problem. If we accept the analogy of sharing and seeking to express our experiences in various ways as the most efficacious means of deepening our appreciation and securing lasting, even if inadequate, effects, then too much silence, pursing of lips, and Anglo-Saxon refusal to become emotionally involved or concerned about the deepest things of life which others may wish to share with us, or ask us to share with them, can be far from helpful, and even far from Christian.

As Christians we believe that God wants to share the deepest mysteries of his own life with us, and that the sending of his Son into our world and into our personal lives is to enable us to receive his revelations about himself and to respond to that invitation. If he wishes so to share with us the mystery of his own life it seems that we should be willing to share with others the mysteries of our own hearts. Our natural desire not to upset others may not always be an adequate excuse for our reticence and unwillingness to provide our own ill-formulated reasons for our beliefs. Sometimes we may have an obligation, as St. Paul says, to 'imitate God' and, like him, take the initiative in proclaiming, not imposing, our faith.

A phoney so-called ecumenism has, in recent years, made such initiatives more difficult, especially I think for Catholics. The view is often implied, and sometimes explicitly expressed, that as we are all going the same way our differences are unimportant. The question of truth is seen as secondary to good will, and as good will is postulated for all men in all conditions and walks of life, the implication is that nothing more is needed. Of course, this is a herring of the reddest hue which should not deter us, for if we were to follow such reasoning to its logical conclusions we would find ourselves rejecting the necessity for all dogma and revealed truth, and the Ten Commandments too. The Incarnation would indeed quickly become a myth of someone's imagination, and all objective truth would vanish. For Catholics, dogmatic truths are seen as objective and all-important, but sometimes we do not perhaps reflect sufficiently on what is likely to ensue if we fail in our personal responsibility to make this clear, and if we do not also explain, as best we can, how and why these apparently cerebral dogmas affect our daily lives. Unless we are prepared to make such efforts it is not surprising if the dogmas we say we treasure are regarded as irrelevant by those who do not share our faith. At first sight, belief in the Assumption of Our Lady or the Immaculate Conception may not seem particularly relevant or helpful to us in our efforts to fulfil our daily Christian responsibilities, and maybe no one of the truths we hold should ever be considered in isolation and out of context. Just as the total panoramic view adds to our appreciation of each particular part, and just as analysis of a member of a dead body can never give us a complete understanding of the part it played when it was part of a living whole, so it is with our understanding and appreciation of the truths we hold. Except in context they cannot be fully understood. But the fact remains that all of God's truths have been given to us to help us, even though, at different times in history and at different times in our own personal lives, now this, and now that, truth may seem more important.

For our friends who see our landscape from another point of view, our inarticulate efforts to explain, however inadequately, why and how we find this particular truth is helpful can be vitally important, and of course it is always important for ourselves too, as it heightens our own appreciation. There will always remain high mysteries in our faith, and dark places which we have never fully explored in the inner recesses of our soul, until the light of the risen Christ reveals all in heaven. Till then we need the courage to go on searching.

The pusillanimous who refuses to speak about the truth because he does not want even to seem to impugn the good faith of others shows little respect for the integrity or the intelligence of his fellow men, who deserve to be preserved from the disasters which the abolition of all moral and doctrinal standards inevitably involves. Unfortunately, whilst most people recognize that moral standards are important—even though they may dispute as to what they should be—the importance of doctrinal truth is increasingly regarded as irrelevant for the needs of modern man. Perhaps those who experience its importance in their own lives may have a more serious obligation than they realize, not necessarily to teach those who do not share their views, but to share with others who are sympathetic some of their own personal vision. In this matter I would think most of us sin more by omission than by commission; not wanting to impose our views nor upset our friends, nor to interfere and meddle with what is not our concern, we refrain from sharing those truths which help us, or sharing our difficulties about truths which we believe and know should help us. If we could refrain from being caught up in the teacher–taught relationship, and confine our activities to sharing both what we love and what we have perhaps failed to incorporate into our lives, we could, it seems to me, avoid the dilemma which paralyses us and prevents our doing the good we are called upon to do. Our lives would be enriched and our personal faith deepened by sharing our faith. Treated in this way ecumenism would certainly enrich the lives of everyone, for it would encourage us all to grow in our knowledge and love of our faith, not as it is in the textbooks, but as it has to be lived in our daily lives.

This also means, as I may not have sufficiently stressed, that we must become appreciative listeners, that we must allow others to tell us their insights in their own way, and really try to understand what it is which sparks off their vision. We have all met those tiresome bores who, searching for an audience, drive us into the corner of a room where we are trapped, unable to escape unless we spill our tea or are rescued by a kindly hostess. Of course she may leave us in our corner, deciding it is time we were fed a little of our own medicine. But the willingness to listen and to learn, to climb higher up the mountain track and see one's favourite view as others see it from a slightly different viewpoint, may be enormously rewarding. Our attention is called, perhaps, to the cloud round the base of the mountain which, like so many of the mysteries of our faith, provides us with further insights into the inadequacy of our present perceptions and the transcending majesty of God. A little further grounding in humility seldom comes amiss; and if we have to admit that this is an aspect of the love and wisdom of God to which we had not before perhaps paid sufficient attention, all the better.

The Scriptures above all are the Living Word of God, and can and should be read and re-read—not necessarily with a concordance at our elbow, but certainly with a prayer in our heart that our eyes may be further opened, so that we can see and thank God more fully for that never-ending wonder of his revelation of himself to us in his creation, in his Son, and in his children whom we meet day by day. To share by listening is often more difficult than to point out to others the things we personally love and seem to have discovered for ourselves.

Perhaps this is a lesson we could learn from many natural

mothers who have had to learn it by hard experience, and from Mary, the Mother of God, who kept all those things she did not understand and pondered them in her heart, until such time as they produced fruit in due season.

10 Friendship

I

Most university chaplains receive letters from fond parents worried when their sons and daughters go up to university for the first time in the family history. The parents are fearful about what may happen. They know a career and future happiness are at stake. How better can their children be helped than through the chaplain?

He may indeed be of assistance, but his influence is likely to be comparatively unimportant. Most people, particularly the young, are more easily influenced by their peers than by other age-groups. If the students are in digs, hostels, halls of residence, or anywhere where they have good friends, they will probably be happy. If they are happy they are unlikely to come to serious harm. The ones about whom parents, and chaplains too, should worry are those who are unhappy. Sometimes forced to live in appalling digs, always cold, spending much of their time and money feeding the ever-hungry gas or electric meters, ravenous themselves and badly fed on soggy pie at night and cold sandwiches for breakfast, no wonder they are unhappy and that their work suffers. For such students there will be strong temptations to alleviate their loneliness by drink, drugs, or anything which will take their minds off their present discontents. They need good friends when the going is difficult.

The problem is not of course confined to university students or those at polytechnics. All who live away from home encounter similar problems. Within an industrialized society we are all frequently uprooted and find ourselves surrounded by people whom we do not know, and this makes us more conscious of our need for friends. Precisely because the environment in which we are forced to live is not of our own choosing, we need someone with whom we can discuss our deepest thoughts, our haunting worries, and lay to rest those skeletons which pursue us in our dreams. Maybe we can then even sketch out the visions we have, but which, unless articulated and forced to face the bright light of day, may well become the ghosts of what might have been, which will in their turn pursue us through our lives. We need someone with whom we can fence and fight mock battles and agree to differ, and so train ourselves for the grim world outside. Someone whom we can invite into our inner sanctum, and who will invite us into his. Mutual trust, with the drawbridges down and the outer ramparts razed to the ground, is essential. The small child who defined a friend as someone who knows you well, and still loves you, was surely not far off the mark.

We read about men like St. Augustine and St. Thomas More and St. Edmund Campion and Cardinal Newman who, in the early crises of their lives, when they were still not clear as to where they should go, or what they should do, were deeply indebted to their friends. So too of course were several of the Apostles, so this was nothing new. For most people, the basic problem is always the same: where to meet such people with whom we can share our basic assumptions and ideals, and get the encouragement we all know we need?

Sometimes we have to wait upon events. General Gordon wrote to his sister: 'We are pianos, events play upon us.' There was in him something of the mystic and maybe the fatalist, but he had already done all that he could do. But to wait upon events and fail to do what lies in our own power would be sorry advice to give to those who seek and cannot find the friendships they need. Much, perhaps all, will depend upon our mental attitudes: what we expect from life and from each other; what we are prepared to give and what we are prepared to receive are equally important. Too often one meets lonely people who wait and wait, and say 'we will see what happens'; and nothing does, or ever will, unless they make it happen. Opportunities may come unasked, but more often they have to be created.

I was very struck once in a city in the USA by the fact that everyone I met was a member of at least one club. There seemed to be innumerable clubs catering for every taste, where like-minded people could easily foregather. A young English couple who were staying there for a year or two complained they had no friends. They had never even tried to join one of the clubs, or I'm sure their story would have been very different. In England, a dog or a pram used to be one of the best ways of making friends. A common interest, in gardens, in football, or in beer may work equally well. A willingness to help with the washing-up after a social event in a Chaplaincy or church hall used to be an almost infallible way of making friends, especially for those shy people who had little to say when they fist met strangers. The initiative lies with us.

II

In recent times the Catholic Church has followed a path already blazed by other Churches and placed a new emphasis on the importance of friendships as a means of bringing our faith more deeply into our lives and transforming our social contacts into friendship in the Lord. Before the Second Vatican

Council many parish retreats and missions started with a
rousing sermon in which we were encouraged, like Moses, to
climb up, ever upwards, through fog and mist to meet our
God. 'Lord that I may know myself, that I may know Thee',
was the prayer most often put upon our lips. A very good
prayer too, but emphasizing only one aspect of our lives. We
live in a world of people, and it is through them that Christ
encourages us to come to himself. In his scene of the final
judgement he is emphatic, as elsewhere, that 'as you did it to
one of the least of these my brethren, you did it to me'.

The strongly individualistic tradition of much pre-Vatican
spirituality as it seeped through in Anglo-Saxon cultures was,
as we can now see, influenced by the traditional nineteenth-
century public school morality which sought to strengthen the
moral fibres of the young. They were trained to stand alone.
The stoics did no less, and many others too, otherwise admirable people, who sought salvation through their strength of
will. Pelagius was perhaps the most famous of them all. He is
said to have come from Britain, and it was against his particular heresy that St. Augustine, with his love for his friends and
his recognition of his own need for human friendship,
inveighed so bitterly. He had to insist that faith is a gift of God;
that we can only go to God if his grace first draws us; that we
can, with the grace which he will always give us, dispose
ourselves. But the idea so often given, tht it all depends upon
us, as though by our own unaided efforts we could go to
heaven, is wholly wrong.

It was in order to underwrite positively what had always
been part of the Christian tradition that the Vatican Council
stressed the importance of the local community. To those
brought up in another, non-Catholic and perhaps non-
Christian, tradition, this emphasis sounded strange and
mildly threatening, even unmanly, suggesting as it did that we
could not cope alone. To those who had already lived out most
of their lives before the Council opened, the communitarian
aspect of the new liturgy was difficult to swallow.

In England, many of a more conservative mind thought that

the socialist tradition had still to prove its worth, and regarded it with suspicion; the thought that such views, which were often regarded with both fear and derision, should have taken root in, and perhaps taken over, their own beloved Church was not unnaturally regarded with dismay.

If only the penny catechism had said, as it well might have said, that a strong sense of community is one of the marks of the Church, many troubles would never have arisen. It was so clearly true of the early Church that it hardly needed saying, had it not been forgotten. All the letters of St. Paul take it for granted: it is in and through the local community that he expects the Church to flourish and influence the world around it.

The medieval churches, the city guilds, and the local customs of pre-Reformation England show how that tradition lasted for many years. The great monasteries, with their granges spread up and down the country, expected their men to come home when their work was done. They were the living embodiment of the importance of the religious community. They were almost too successful. The concept of community became so identified with monks and nuns that with the destruction of the monasteries the concept of a spiritual community was almost lost to sight.

The strong individualism of Protestant England took over, especially in the Churches, and the concept of community was reserved for the village, for the Dissenters, and for such guilds as survived. Primarily the local community was seen as a useful social adjunct connected with bazaars, fêtes, and jumble sales to raise money for the school, or the needs of the parish, or some other good cause. It was no longer thought of as an essential in the spiritual lives of the faithful.

III

In the early sixties, when the notion of the Eucharistic community started to gather momentum, I was amazed to find that what sounded like a pious theory actually worked in practice. The students at the university were allowed to have Mass in the middle of the day, or in the evening, with only slight fasting regulations for those wishing to go to Holy Communion; and almost immediately what had been a good social club became an embryonic Eucharistic community. The Mass took on a social dimension it had never had before, and so too did the faith of those who shared it. Deep friendships were made between those who had so suddenly been encouraged to pray together.

Laws created to safeguard liberties can strangle lives; structures created to embody a mission can harden and stultify what they should be promoting. Endless adjustments are always necessary. Persecutions in the past have freed the mission of the Church from structures which were embrangling it. The Second Vatican Council was concerned with such a freeing of the Spirit, and not primarily with laws or structures. But to live the life of the Spirit we need support, and if we do not get it from our culture nor from an institution, then we need it from our friends who share our deepest ideals. It is within the Eucharistic community that such friendships can most easily be formed, shibboleths destroyed, and a Christian impact on an increasingly pagan and often secretly hostile secular environment be strengthened.

Central to such friendships and such communities is the Eucharist, which incorporates all that we both strive to attain and wish to express. 'I am the Vine, you are the branches' reminds us that our lives are only fruitful if they are grounded in Christ; 'as you did it to one of the least of these my brethren, you did it to me' reminds us that we find Christ in and through our fellow men, and we shall meet our fellow men more deeply if we meet them in and through Christ. 'Just as each of our bodies has several parts and each part has a separate function, so all of us, in union with Christ, form one body, and as parts of it we belong to each other.'

No longer can we separate our social and religious obligations. At every step the two interpenetrate. Our horizontal and vertical obligations meet in the cross and share our life. A personal love of Christ is vital—or our human friendships will suffer, and lose their finest and deepest quality; with the result that our faith becomes an arid philosophical system, with all the hard lines which that entails.

I remember meeting an old friend once by chance on a country path. He asked me, 'What are you going to do for Christ?' I was somewhat taken aback and at a loss for words. At that time I had already taken my vows but was not then, if I remember aright, a priest. I was under vows of obedience. What was there left for me to do? My friend pressed me further; that is what friends are for, and he was right. St. Paul spoke of the love of Christ as urging him and compelling him, like the hound of heaven. Not enough to wait and see what happens. We have to seize the initiative when and where we can, and then new opportunities occur at every step.

IV

It is the same with all friendships, human and divine. They are never static, but ever vibrant, pulsing, ever demanding, growing, living, involving all that we are and all we hope to be. They have to embrace all aspects of our life, and call for time and energy and sacrifice, and some confrontations too. Only at our peril can we take them for granted. Too many broken marriages, and discouraged people who have lost their faith, bear tragic witness to this truth that love, both human and divine, has to be fed so that it grows stronger, or it will surely die.

If God gave us—as I think we must agree he did—the gift of laughter, humour, and joy, so that when we are happy we must surely smile, then all of that must find expression in our friendships with one another and, equally important, in what used to be called our spiritual lives: our friendship with Christ. It is part of our human heritage, but an aspect of our lives we do not so readily associate with God.

The puritanical strain is well and deeply entrenched in our

mentality. We would willingly believe that if we turned ourselves into prophets of doom and gloom, and uttered harsh strictures on the ways of the ungodly, like modern Cassandras, we might be considered holy; at least such sentiments from apparently good and holy men do not surprise us, even if we think them mistaken. We know that that is not our vocation, nor are we holy, so why should we worry. But deep in our system is the belief that serious matters should only be considered with due solemnity, as though that were a safer way to God. I do not wish to advocate frivolity; but I think we should be ourselves, and that it is as human beings that God wants our love. Our friends expect no less. Why then should we exclude God from that side of life which we enjoy most?

This is a curious quirk we have which St. Thomas More was quick to point out, as did many of the English martyrs, but it was not well received. Jokes by those condemned to die were considered quite unseemly. Few would have approved of St. Charles Borromeo who, asked what he would do if when playing chess he was told he was about to die, replied that he would finish his game; nor of a friend of mine who as he lay dying tried to sing *Box and Cox* with his brother. They had sung it together since they were boys, and he had long since tried to prepare himself for death. The good St. John Kemple at Hereford asked for a last pipe and and last drink with the his gaoler before he was put to death. Men like these could and did enjoy their games, their songs, their drinks, their jokes, and their pipes as part of their preparation for heaven.

Belloc, of course, in the thirties ranted and railed against the puritanism of England; but after all he was so Gallic in his approach that his scale of values, with his love of laughter and wine, was considered slightly odd—and now, alas, he is fast becoming quite unknown. G. K. Chesterton also had much to say about this, and said it extraordinarily well, but we have not seen his like again—a man of vast proportions truly rooted in basic common sense.

They were following a tradition not only of the martyrs but of men like Cardinal Newman, who loved to stress that our faith is above all concerned with the presence of persons: the indwelling of the Blessed Trinity, the presence of God in the Blessed Sacrament, and in one another. The way we love our friends cannot be so very different from the way we love God's Son. We love as we are, for that is all we have to give and we must give it all. Humour, laughter, and joy are qualities which help us to see things in perspective, especially ourselves, so that the weight of the world is firmly lifted from our shoulders and placed where it belongs. When we are happy, we find new depths within ourselves and others; and we can weep for joy, and laugh when we are sad. Contrasts and contradictions, and paradoxes too, are as important in our lives as simple logic or an iron will—though these last have their uses.

Theology and pure reason, like simple logic, are not enough. They can so easily lead to rationalism, so that we are worldly wise but quite cut off from God; so can devotion by itself lead us to superstition, and a life lived on emotion. Our faith needs our reason, for we must give what we are; and our reason needs our faith, or we shall stay earth-bound forever; and perhaps both need the gift of laughter and a smile to keep the perspective right. All that God made is good and given to enrich our lives, if we can only use it aright. To exclude from our love of God so much that we love and treasure in our lives, and above all in our human friendships, would be very odd. Our friends and laughter too help us to God.

For most of us our happiness is not a solemn matter. It is a pinnacle, a high point in our lives, and one, we hope, recurring all the time. How odd it is that we seek God and talk to him when we are lost in the mists of time, and forget him on the peaks. The Psalmist knew much better, and in his prayers included all that makes up man.

Most of us find it more difficult to receive than to give. In the early sixties I remember a member of the German Federal Government, who was responsible for providing aid to the Developing Countries, opening his speech with the remark: 'Whenever I am walking down a street and see someone I know crossing the road so as to avoid meeting me, I always ask myself what benefits my country has recently conferred on his.' He already knew well what has now become an axiom of our times, that it is by conferring benefits that many enemies are made, and friendships put under more strains than they can stand. The giver may be over-paternalistic, condescending, or even imperialistic, as though gratitude could be bought; but the main reason for the antagonism is the unwillingness of the recipient to enter into debt and lose his freedom. To receive gracefully, maintain a friendship and not feel humiliated is not easy with our human friends, nor yet with God.

To face the fact of our dependence on his creative love is the beginning of wisdom, for then truth can enter our hearts. The Eucharist is concerned, as its name implies, with giving thanks. To many of an older generation the new Mass, where the community is gathered round the bare altar, is very unattractive. Gone is the mystique which once enthralled. A new quality is demanded, as we try to praise the Lord. Gone too, for many, is the sense that in the same way, all over the world, the whole Church is united in one sacrifice of love, praise and thanksgiving.

Underneath the changes, the reality is unchanged. We still do all we used to do; but we are encouraged to do more. 'No longer do I call you servants . . . but I have called you friends.' It is in and through the Mass that our friendships with Christ and with one another are fostered and fed with a quality which, left to ourselves, we could not hope to offer. It is as friends in the Lord that we can help each other. It is not normally good for man to be alone, and when he is alone then he is called to share in the loneliness of Christ upon his Cross. Sacrifices which must be endured can be endured, for others as well as for ourselves, and so will enrich their lives as well as ours. In heaven all loneliness is gone, and in God we truly find each other in new and I would think even more marvellous ways. 'In his body lives the fullness of divinity, and in him you too find your own fulfilment.'

11 Angels' wings?

Do you ever dream of Angels' wings? When I was very young my mother, at that time a recent convert to Catholicism, embroidered a garden scene with a magnificent herbaceous border, a mass of colour, and across the lawn there was a saying which read:

> God sends his Angels in our great distress
> But little ones come in and out all day.

As a child I remember many visitors remarking on it and liking it. I thought it rather sentimental but never said so, as I knew my mother was fond of it. Only in later life did I recall it with affection and begin to understand what it was all about. By then I was in my studies for the priesthood, and Angels were still very much 'in' in Catholic theology, nor was there much difficulty made about the value of devotion to Guardian Angels, even though the theologians might disagree about the quality of the theological mode or certitude which was to be attached to the doctrine. I do not think we were really too concerned as to whether we were being looked after by the particular personal providence of God, to which Cardinal Newman had such devotion, or whether a special Angel had been deputed by him to look after us. In practice, however God worked it out, we were all convinced that there was a special vocation to which we were each called, and that God's graces could be relied upon to reach us.

I suppose that it was this that sparked off my interest in the wings of Angels. I am sure that some learned man must have done much research on this matter, probably the theologians somewhere have worked on it too, and even to the casual observer there is something fascinating about the wings of Angels. They vary enormously as depicted in art through the ages.

When I was at Campion Hall there was an Abyssinian Madonna which Evelyn Waugh, when he was a war correspondent, had brought back for the Hall. The Abyssinian Angels really regarded their function as protective, and had very large wings with sharp points at the end—woe betide anyone who fell foul of them. But the German Austrian Angels of the sixteenth century were more like feathered birds, downy, and clearly their wings were designed to help them to fly to the highest heavens. A little Chinese Angel seemed to have put on his wings, the removable variety, for the occasion. He was shown as flying with a very special purpose, like one of those determined drivers one sometimes sees, who give the impression that they are so intent upon their purpose that they would rather die than surrender their rights. This Chinese Angel was clearly engaged upon a special mission, and making rapid progress against strong head winds. In the porch of the church in Malmesbury there are Anglo-Saxon carvings with Angels who have magnificent wings, solid affairs easily capable of protecting the six Apostles on either side who crouch under them as if they were an enormous umbrella.

In the Scriptures the Angels are given wings so that they can shield us from the wrath of God, and (at a time when wings indicated the greatest possible mobility known to man) come to our assistance at a moment's notice and yet fly back equally quickly to continue their work of worshipping and adoring God for all eternity. They are seen as the messengers of God, intermediaries, whose home is in heaven, but who can always be relied upon to come to our aid and give a lift to our faltering steps.

In the University Chaplaincy where I used to work we had a picture of an Angel with the most extraordinarily large wings protecting Tobias as the two walked together on their pilgrimage to collect the money owing to Tobias's father. In front of them walked the little dog, as recorded in St. Jerome's Vulgate translation of the Bible. It was the Angel, we are told, who introduced Tobias to Sarah and encouraged him to marry her, and after the wedding was over it was the Angel who protected them all the way home, and the little dog, we are told, went ahead of them wagging its tail for joy. According to some variants the little dog should be translated as 'The Lord'. For practical purposes it does not seem to make much difference. One of the purposes of the story is to show God smiling benignly on a young married couple, and also to indicate that their marriage had in a sense been arranged, like all sacramental marriages, in heaven. It seems such a suitable introduction to what we read later at the marriage feast at Cana. Quite clearly Our Lord is really interested in people, and in their human happiness and their personal relationships and human love.

Whenever I attend a Catholic wedding I am reminded that the sacrament of marriage must take place, as St. Paul would have said, before a host of heavenly witnesses. You can think of the whole court of heaven looking down, the grandparents and great-grandparents and all the host of friends. If they loved the young couple when they were on earth, surely they must love them still more now they are in heaven. But you can think too of the Angels with big wings, or the self-effacing Guardian Angels who are getting on with the job. You can, of course, content yourself with recalling the doctrine of the Church, that the sacrament entitles those who receive it to all the graces and strength they will need to be loyal to each other throughout their married life, and that these graces may come to them through Angels, or through the prayers and love of their friends, or in any other way God wishes to send them.

If indeed God sends his Angels, or at least his special graces, in our great distress, we can rest assured that his little ones go in and out through all the day. We may think we are alone, but it is never quite like that. God loves each one of us too much. His graces, or if you prefer it his Angel, or even, for we can appropriate it to ourselves, our Guardian Angel, is always there watching over us so that he can help us rise above our present discontent. Looking towards the goal laid out for us, we need to place our hearts where our hopes must surely be, in the infinite loving mercy of an all-loving God. With his wings the Angel can transport us to another world, shield us and protect us, so that with our hearts in Heaven we have renewed courage to face the trials and tribulations of our daily life. We are ever beneath the shadows of their wings. As Francis Thompson said:

> The angels keep their ancient places;—
> Turn but a stone, and start a wing!
> 'Tis ye, 'tis your estrangèd faces,
> That miss the many-splendoured thing.

12   Gratitude

I

OFTEN we think of gratitude as 'count your blessings', and we acknowledge them. We enumerate our presents in our fingers and tick them off to make sure no one is forgotten. It would never do to fail to thank our friends.

I am reminded of a small boy I used to know who was between four and a half and five. His parents doted on him, for he was their only child and they would have liked more. They showered gifts upon him, and in his nursery the cupboards were so full of toys the doors would not stay shut. The floor was littered with bricks, bits of Lego, mini-cars and fierce-looking animals on wheels. Many were broken, but some with a little ingenuity and considerable brute force could be made to work. The walls were covered with those colourful hangings specially designed to please the young. They also enchanted most of the older generation. Throughout the house you came across the loving care and thoughtfulness of the fond parents for their beloved son. The toys spilled out from the nursery into the hall, stairway and kitchen; they overflowed from the garage on to the back lawn. To have a bath in such a house was an experience you shared with a variety of ducks, boats and rubber dolls which floated round and round and seemed to survive when you inadvertently sat on one or crushed it against the side.

Sleeping and waking, washing and eating, indoors and out of doors, you came across the vigilance and untiring energy and love of the parents who were, alas, spoiling their little boy. It was hard to see what more they could have done, but they might, with profit, have done considerably less. They skimped their holidays and never went to parties on their own. Their child was the centre of their lives, and their car an extension of the nursery. Giving him all they could, they wanted to see him happy and hear his delight. They realized that it was they, and not their child, who had the most cause to be grateful.

The parents' lives had been enriched through the birth of their child, whom they had badly wanted for many years. Their lives now had that added purpose which it had not had before, and which it badly needed if their marriage was to survive. They did what they could to enrich their young son's life—but the superabundance of toys was almost a distraction, which veiled rather than revealed the intensity of their love.

I was often reminded of another child of poorer parents, who had few toys. When he was given a large brown paper parcel for his birthday he so much enjoyed the anticipation he experienced as he tried to open it that he almost ignored the gift inside. It was the string, the brown paper, and the cardboard box which held his attention. These he knew he was free to destroy as he willed. The string belonged to him and could be tied into knots; the paper could be torn at will and crumpled into balls and thrown this way and that; the box he kicked around as if it were a football and it provided him with fun. He knew these trappings were unimportant, but they had been

received from his fond parents, or the services which the patients received in the hospital ward.

The wonderful thing about the boy with no arms or legs, and about my blind friend, was that they could see in their afflictions a gift from God which enabled them to do something far greater with their lives than they would have been able to do without them. They saw their weaknesses and deformities as positive helps. On the natural plane they had to try to compensate for their physical inadequacies, and in any event they would have tried to do that. The boy would almost certainly have been bound to become an extrovert if he was to survive at all. The blind man would naturally have become more perceptive than those who did not need to rely so heavily on their other senses. But both went further than that. They did not just tolerate their difficulties, they did not merely resign themselves to their inevitable fate. They accepted the new conditions with joy, because they saw them as positive enabling gifts from God.

That would seem to be a difficult lesson to learn. Sometimes one meets old people whom no one wants to know. They feel themselves unwanted, lonely, useless, they feel that they have nothing left to give—or so they think. But they are wrong. Their weakness may be the physical weakness of old age, or the mental feebleness of those who have no friends and are unutterably alone. Their weakness may be the aftermath of a life of sin, selfishness, and greed. We all have within us our own private hell which, over a long life or a short one, we may have built into ourselves. To see these afflictions as of any positive help often seems quite impossible. Many people, in my experience, resign themselves to the situation they have brought upon themselves, they bear it with heroic fortitude; but they do not appreciate that there is any positive good to be drawn from the afflictions.

Yet we are told repeatedly that our gratitude to God should embrace all things: the world in which we live as it is at the present time, and as we have helped to make it or mar it through our lives. The world within our hearts and the world outside is the world with which we must be concerned. 'All things work together unto good for them that love God.' Our faith teaches us that God is omnipotent, and can draw good out of evil once it has been repented. Forgiven sins are stepping-stones to God. The past, however terrible it may have been, can be brought under the mantle of God's love for us and help us now in our present situation. There is indeed for all of us much for which we should be grateful: our present, our past, and our hopes for the future too.

God speaks to us in different ways, and his gifts take different forms. The problem for most of us is to recognize them for what they are and this we can only do if our hearts are right, in sympathy with his. *Cor ad cor loquitur*—heart speaks to heart. The language, the nature of the gifts or even of the service are increasingly unimportant once the basic vital relationship has been established. If our hearts are in tune with his, we can count our blessings all our days.

Hopkins saw the world as the word of God, as his expression, so that everything we see or experience in ourselves is part of that dynamic whole. He saw even the physical world around us as having been affected by the fact that God became man so that the world has now taken on a 'tug', a 'pitch', a 'direction' it never had before. It is indeed for Hopkins the poet, as for the mystical St. Paul, filled with the grandeur of God which all men should be able to see and which should lead us all to him.

Alas, most of us, as well as the people with whom we live and love, find this impossible to grasp. The reasons may lie outside our personal control. In his excellent biography of St. Augustine Peter Brown pointed out how this blindness was true even of that great saint before his conversion. Many men with whom St. Augustine consorted were quite willing to believe that in the beginning was the word, for they did not think that this truth affected their personal lives. They were willing to look with kindly toleration on organized religion and its devotees. They enjoyed their own spiritual independence and their freedom to indulge in 'honest doubt'. Unsullied by the drudgery which commitment necessarily involves, they were free to stand on the touch-line and applaud the efforts of the men of faith. They had no gratitude, for they did not understand that the peace and freedom and happiness which they considered the prerogative of all good men was in reality the spin-off from that world of faith which at other times, when it so suited them, they ignored, decried, and sometimes despised.

Only when they were called upon to believe that 'the Word was made Flesh' did their attitude have to change. When confronted they could not escape some measure of involvement, whatever they might do. They could not remain unscathed, however much they might wish their status of honest onlookers to remain the same. They had to choose, and, if they allowed this new truth to enter their lives, they found they were committed to receiving more than the gifts and grandeur of God in his creation, more than the fruits of his service as it came to them in his providence over all things. Acceptance of that truth meant they were transported, not so unlike Ezekiel carried by the roots of his hair, into a different world where they became something more important even than becoming the members of a team.

The child who received gifts from his parents was not as a result very deeply involved; the gifts had a transient, impersonal quality, even though they pointed to the love of the parents. The patients in the hospital ward received the cheerful devoted services of the nurses, and found that their gratitude had to extend beyond one or two persons to the whole body of men and women whose lives were structured so that the patients could be helped. Their gratitude had to express something of that same quawity of service if it was to be genuine at all; the gift had dug deeper into their being. But when St. Augustine found he had to believe that 'the Word was made Flesh' he soon discovered he had accepted more than a notional truth into his life.

The gifts or toys which God showers upon us point to his loving kindness and concern; the devoted service which we receive from others, and which indicates how God is always working through people and through things on our behalf, still has a transient quality, like the clothes we wear. These things point to something deeper and more permanent in our lives; but for the most part we are probably seldom aware of that deeper and truer significance.

But once we believe that 'the Word was made Flesh', these transient truths become embedded in our being and a new dimension opens in our lives. The boy with no arms and legs, and the blind man, had appreciated this deeper truth. Because of the Incarnation the world was now a different place, and had a unity it had never had before. No longer could men be considered as so many disparate beings, for now they were all called to a share in the one life of Christ.

Before his conversion St. Augustine could say of himself: 'I chattered away as someone in the know . . . had I continued to be such an expert, I had gone to my own destruction.' *Peritus, periturus.* He had thought that intellectual arguments plumbed the depths of man, and had been blind to the ultimate realities which circumscribe our lives.

Something very similar happened to Cardinal Newman, as he explains in his *Apologia*. 'I was beginning to prefer intellectual excellence to moral; I was drifting in the direction of the Liberalism of the day'—which put its faith in reason as the ultimate arbiter of our destinies. The truth of the Incarnation brought home to him the fact that Christianity was not a philosophy but a 'substantive message from above'. In the Incarnation, as Hopkins said, 'God gave things a forward and perpetual motion'.

It was this deeper truth which enabled the boy with no arms and legs, and the blind man, to be grateful to God for their frightful deformities. Convinced that they were called on to share in the life of Christ, they easily understood that they were also called on to share in his work, to share in something greater than themselves and in a more substantive way than mere words would suggest, more substantive even than the way the individual nurses shared in the work of the hospital

ward. They were being called on to be more than members of a
team of like-minded men fired with the same ideals. Their
suffering, because the Word was made Flesh, was a call to
share in the redemptive work of Christ. In some mysterious
way, although we are redeemed by Christ alone, God can and
does use and value our contributions which we can make in
virtue of our baptism, 'in and with and through Christ', and
this gives our individual lives an immediate point and a long-
term purpose and a richness we cannot hope to comprehend,
for they belong now to Christ who is God as well as Man.

St. Paul in his letter to the Thessalonians thanked God
because they had received 'God's message . . . for what it
really is, God's message, and not some human thinking' and
as a result, as he said, 'it is still a living power among you who
believe it'. It is because of that 'living power' which a Christian
receives from Christ that we are encouraged to 'give thanks
always'.

It is that 'always' which we need to ponder. It is easy for us
to thank God for the gifts we have received and which remind
us of what he wants to give. It is equally easy for us to thank
him for his devoted service on which we rely all through our
lives. But the gifts and the service are given to prepare our
hearts to accept that deeper and more wonderful gift of himself
which he wants to give us so that we may share his life, his
work, his suffering, his death, and his risen life in Heaven.
'That they may all be one; even as thou, Father, art in me, and I
in thee, that they also may be in us.'

V

This does of course presuppose the gift of faith, and here we
should perhaps remember that one of the safest criteria for
establishing truth is not reasons, for mysteries elude them, but
coherence between thought, heart, and life, leading to an
integrity which, like the visible world around us, points as its

only explanation beyond where unaided human reason can lead us. That final leap, the leap of faith, is where God draws us: that is why he speaks to us in different haunting ways. We should indeed remember his past mercies, for he never ceases to communicate with us, and seeks to draw us on.

We do not always hear him; but those who, like the crippled boy and my blind friend, listened to his message and incorporated it into their lives were enabled to give a witness to the truth denied to lesser men. Their crosses gave them high pulpits from which, by the integrity of their lives of faith, inexplicable on purely human terms, they could compel attention and draw men to Christ. Of recent years there seem to have been many such wonderful men of different faiths, for whom we should thank God.

One of the results of the Ecumenical Movement for which we also should be grateful has been the introduction into liturgical language of words—especially Old Testament words—which still sound strange to our ears. The word 'covenant', in particular, was a word which Catholics, so far as I can recollect, seldom used in pre-Vatican II days. In this context, it is an important word indicating an even more important truth. It brings home to us the faithfulness of God to his contractual promises: the covenant with Abraham, the covenant on Sinai and the covenant with David, and the personal relationships which ensue and illustrate God's love for his chosen people as Father, Mother, Shepherd etc. Today we have Canon Four in the Mass to highlight a truth we have always known, but which always needs to be more deeply rooted in our hearts. It helps to remind us why we should be giving thanks to God all through our lives.

When we reflect on what it means—God's promises all through Old Testament times, the fulfilment of his promises in sending us his Son, then no wonder St. Paul writes to the Colossians:

> . . . giving thanks to the Father,
> who has qualified us to share
> in the inheritance of the saints in light.

He has delivered us from the dominion of darkness
and transferred us to the kingdom of his beloved Son,
in whom we have redemption,
the forgiveness of sins.

He is the image of the invisible God,
the first-born of all creation;
for in him all things were created, in heaven and on earth,
visible and invisible . . .

. . . all things were created
through him and for him.
He is before all things,
and in him all things hold together.

He is the head of the body, the church;
he is the beginning,
the first-born from the dead,
that in everything he might be pre-eminent.

For in him all the fulness of God was pleased to dwell,
and through him to reconcile to himself all things,
whether on earth or in heaven,
making peace by the blood of his cross.

God has been faithful to his promises. His Son has fulfilled
his promise too in not leaving us orphans but sending us his
Holy Spirit to teach us, and to be with us in a new way. More
than enough blessings to count and send us off to sleep.

Even in apparent disaster, in the hell of Dachau, in the
ruination of all our hopes and aspirations, in the mysterious
cruel and unnecessary sufferings of the innocent, in the folly
and stupidity of man, in our loneliness when we are tempted
to think we are no longer needed, in our consciousness of
failure through our own folly and impatience, in our misery
when we suddenly realize in some distressing way how far we
are from loving or trusting God, in our worries about our dead
loved one, in our frustrations when we cannot do what we had
hoped to do, in our sense of isolation when our friends leave

us and we seem destined to live out our lives apart, in our incipient feelings of despair when we can no longer see any glimmerings of joy or hope on the horizon, in our pain and sufferings which seem destined to go on for ever, in our inability to recapture the lost visions of happier days, in our lethargy and apathy when we seem more dead than alive, when we feel the whole world is closing in upon us and we shall soon be quite forgotten and that we are lost for ever deep in a pit with the sides crumbling, in our consciousness of our sinful nature and of our own very personal sins, we can and should try to thank God. When it seems quite impossible—then is the time to cry out 'Lord I am not worthy' and let his grace and love enter in; then is the time for us to join Christ in his agony in the garden and give thanks and put our trust in him. When we are weak—and if we are not weak at times like these when are we weak?—then, through our faith in Christ, we become strong. It is by and through our crosses—and if these are not crosses what are?—and our afflictions (whether made by ourselves or others) that he is always calling us to give more of ourselves to him through love and trust, and so to share more fully in his work for men. Without the crosses we would not be capable of giving half as much. The crosses are enabling gifts which do more than increase our perception. They seem to break us down—they do break us down—so that more of Christ can enter in.

He loves us too much to let us live complacent lives in a fools' paradise which, too late, we would regret for ever. The present is too important for him to allow us to waste our lives like children hypnotized by a new toy. Our gratitude is not then just for ephemeral things which can be counted on fingers, nor yet for his loving providence which sustains us through our lives, but for that gift he gives us of himself, and for that invitation which he offers us afresh anew each day to share more fully in his life and work for men. Through faith we thank him for our crosses, for they enrich our lives. They enable us too to show compassion for our fellow men, if only we can have some of that integrity which was so manifest in the boy with no arms and legs and my blind friend. Their lives, and those of all good men, should inspire us through faith to thank God for all his gifts and graces, and for all those apparently disabling and disagreeable deformities and things which we do not like, but which allow him to enter more fully into our lives. At all times, unceasingly, we can and should thank God.

.

13   The old

I<small>T</small> is always a pleasure to drive visitors from overseas round the English countryside. They are appreciative, there is so much to see, and they ask interesting questions. Recently I was told of one young au pair girl who had inquired what a building was and, on being informed that it was a home for old people, asked what that might be. When she learnt that we so often segregate the old from the rest of the community she buried her face in her hands as she exclaimed, 'How horrible'. The fact that the old were well cared for, that they had heating and lighting and even a warden to care for them if they were suddenly taken ill, did nothing to console the poor girl from overseas.

'In my country,' she explained, 'we have always had a great respect for the old. We do not look on them as people who have become mere onlookers on life, as people who have no more to give. We look on them far more as natural leaders; their wisdom and experience . . .' she hesitated, her English was not too good, 'would venerate be the right word, or is that reserved for God alone?' She went on hurriedly to say how in her country it was normal for old people to be cared for by their relatives, and how much she felt she herself owed to her grandmother who had lived with them at her home all through her own lifetime.

I was reminded of an American university where rooms for the old had been built on top of the student hostels. I had asked if the old did not feel segregated and unwanted, but was told they loved it. The students, who often got tired of living only with their own age group, welcomed them. Apparently it was not too noisy—maybe the old were deaf—but I suspect the students respected their need for relative peace. They lived their own lives, and after a time both young and old found to their mutual surprise that they were needed. Many friendships were made. Some of the old attended lectures and seminars and even did exams, and I was told they did surprisingly well. I did not have time to visit the hostels myself, but one of the Vice-Presidents assured me that he thought it was an experiment which, though still in its infancy, was working well. I do not know what my young au pair girl would have thought of that, but at least it seemed a happier solution than many which have been attempted in England.

I wonder if it is the planning authorities, or the architects, or the economic squeeze, or the relatives who have been responsible for trying to bury the old long before they are dead, or should one blame the sick music-hall jokes about the mother-in-law?

Today it is accepted that we all need roots, and this at a time when more people than ever before in the history of the world have been forced to leave their own country by arbitrary governments, or to leave the towns or villages, where they and so many of their ancestors have lived since time immemorial, because of economic necessity or the whim of some planning authority.

To me it was indescribably sad to hear, when staying on a farm in Western Ireland, the mother of a family of six say of them—as if they were puppies—there is only a living here for one, the rest will all have to leave. From an economic point of view I am sure she was right, but all those children were, and forever would be, rooted in the Kerry peninsula—and the Irish have such strong roots that, wherever they go, it has rightly been said, that they carry a bit of Ireland with them. It was the young in this case who would be forced to leave the old behind them, to their mutual sorrow.

Would I could say that we were all equally conscious of the human impoverishment which comes to young and old when they are segregated. Today, when we need all the security possible to face the trials and uncertainties of life, we are for the most part deprived of that added sense of security and belonging which comes from doting grandparents or doting grandchildren, and which complements and deepens what the parents can give.

When I was a chaplain to university students I was at first surprised how deep an influence on them was still being exercised by their grandparents. Never having had any myself, I may be over-sentimentalizing what to the casual observer seems to be one of the most fruitful of human relationships.

Something analogous used to be normal in most religious houses, where one would meet one or two very old priests and brothers. They were not able to do much work, but it was noticeable how all the visitors always wanted to see them, and asked after them, rather as a child asks after his favourite uncle in the hope of being given a chocolate. The special contribution of the old to any religious family group was something intensely personal, not knowledge or even spiritual direction, though they might also be adept at these. They were singled out for their human qualities: they always had time, were available, were never in a hurry, and were so obviously delighted to see you that you realized with a heart-ache how lonely they often were. Without exception they loved children, were interested in you as a person, were full of questions, glad to listen, and, like all of us, glad of a chance to talk. Above all they were often rugged outspoken personalities;

very real. They did not need to wear a mask or pretend—they had lived too long for that, and had nothing much to lose. They could not be labelled as you can label most people who do a job; not eccentrics, they were just normal, friendly, and so rooted in this world and the next that their friendship was always stimulating.

Time and again I have met Jesuits, and many other priests and religious, who told me that they first thought of the priesthood or of the religious life, because they had got to know some old brother in some parish, or school, or retreat house where they had stayed. This seems to be an experience common all over the world, and was especially true in the USA. The old made a unique impact, not only on their religious brethren (a fact which I find is seldom acknowledged), but also on the apostolic mission of the house, though they were not personally involved. If surveys were made, I suspect the influence of old brothers and old priests would far outweigh, in the opinion of most parents and their children, that of the more able teachers and retreat-givers, eloquent preachers, and parish priests. I sometimes wonder if the early middle-aged are not afraid that the old will somehow cramp their style, or reveal their own inadequacies, and whether for similar unarticulated fears, and not solely because of housing problems, young couples so readily agree to sending their own parents to homes where they will be 'comfortable', 'quiet', and 'well looked after'. Is that what they really need? We are all the losers. Too often there seems to be no other solution, but do we give in too easily? I suspect we do.

Early so-called retirement has, of course, made what was already a problem infinitely worse. The prematurely retired are so often seen as having no future, as incapable of making a useful contribution to society, as a burden eating into the financial, medical, social, and housing resources of the community. Despite what is said, it must be difficult to convince the old that they are wanted when all the evidence points the other way; and if they are also sick, then they know that many see them as occupying beds sorely needed by others, and even as ruining the lives of those who look after them. Society needs the young; she does not give many indications today that she thinks the old or the sick provide an essential and positive service to the rest of the community. The very phrase—'a caring community'—is full of overtones that mother knows best, that a long-suffering paternalistic government will, despite all the cries from those who favour euthanasia, not go back on its obligations; but the overtone which comes through most strongly is that the old and weak have nothing positive to contribute to society, except in so far as they are interesting specimens who may increase our medical knowledge of man and what makes him function well or ill.

Yet for the most part the old and sick, despite the odds against them, do not give in. They have enough experience and wisdom to be tolerant of the impatience of youth.

When calling on an old lady of ninety-four I was amazed to find how patient she was. When I had known her well, twenty years earlier whilst working on a parish, she had been looked after by a younger sister. She still was. They had both grown old together gracefully and gratefully, despite physical suffering. From my experience I suspect that in almost every street in England you can meet similar examples of heroic self-sacrifice where people are giving up their lives for one another. Yet it has been my experience that when we meet such people we are conscious that it is we who have been given a great privilege—they help us to see our own lives and troubles in better perspective. As T. S. Eliot said in another context, such people look beyond this 'turning world' of space and time to the 'still point' at the centre, from which the Spirit of Wisdom 'reaches mightily from one end of the earth to the other'.

Again, I often remember a wonderful old lady of ninety-six, widowed for over twenty years, who was cared for by a 'help'. She suffered terribly from arthritis, and was crippled in her chair. The Church of England vicar, a former Catholic priest whom I knew slightly, used to visit her. She was one of his flock, and he so rightly suggested that she might find the *Imitation of Christ* helpful in her sufferings. I had known her for many many years, but had never thought of suggesting that she should read the *Imitation*, which I had known well and loved when I was young. We all need each other. I still think of her wistfully asking me one day, 'Would it be wrong for me to ask Our Lord to take me?' She had lost her son during the war, and longed to see him again. Who could blame her? She died soon after—very peacefully—and was buried in a churchyard overlooking a small lake. Why should so many people, I sometimes angrily ask myself, be deprived of all the wonderful help which the old and very sick can give us?

For the most part they cannot do much physically for their fellow men, but very many of them have led full and interesting lives, and have much wisdom and experience to impart. So too do most other people, and this is not a special charisma of which the old have a monopoly. They are not necessarily wiser or more experienced than those who are younger. Experience and wisdom is a consequence of intelligent reflection rather than of age.

The contribution to society which the old can make in a special way, and usually better than other age groups, lies in their appreciation of the present moment. Sometimes, like all of us, they may by temperament live over-much in the past; sometimes, like the young in heart, they may live over-much in the future; but usually they have learnt to avoid the extremes, and have learnt also to take things as they come.

Our Lord warned St. Peter that a day would come when another would lead him where he did not want to go. Often the old succeed in accepting the physical limitations of old age as they come to them day after day, and the inevitable boredom. Mary Ward used to say that 'God grows in monotony'. The opportunity is certainly there. Some of the old seem to see it, treasure it, and use it aright. To meet such people is more than a privilege; it is an opportunity to learn what time is all about, a lesson which we easily forget and need to re-learn daily throughout our lives. If only we can treasure the value of the present moment we can transform our lives, and maybe introduce a better balance between 'doing' and 'being'. It is a curious paradox of our current civilization that, whilst there is a growing appreciation of the need to inculcate a right use of leisure into the young and the middle-aged, the contribution of the old, who so often have succeeded in getting their values right, is ignored.

We spend much of our life hoping, and waiting for our hopes to be fulfilled, and in so doing we sometimes waste the only time we have. One thinks of people not surprisingly impatient when the bus is late, when an appointment is not kept on time, when life does not follow that order we had planned. To see order and value in waiting and frustration means that we are becoming concerned with something greater than ourselves: our vision is being extended beyond our own personal ambitions, our appreciation deepened to see value and beauty in what is not our own. The job of the old is perhaps very largely to appreciate what the physically more active still can do, to appreciate too what God allows to come their way in pain and frustration and limitations, and to see their own particular role, which can increasingly absorb all their attention, as praising God for everything that is.

When we were novices in Roehampton there were always a number of old men in the community, and many generations of novices will recall some of those men who gladly spent their days in praising God for the wonders and goodness of his creation. To meet such men was a vitally important element in the training of the young. Today too many men are deprived of that inspiration, and it is the young who suffer most. I suppose it is the courage of the old which is infectious: their courage to face the inevitable, deteriorating, and at first sight bleak future can spin off and help the young to find the courage they need to face the unknown, and the middle-aged the courage they need to persevere. Of all the natural virtues this seems to be the one which is most important. It is a virtue we have all met in refugees who, like so many Poles and Hungarians and Pakistanis and West Indians, have had to re-make their lives in an alien culture, and in old age have been compelled to spend much of their time in contemplating the world around them.

Those who have been able to see this as a privileged opportunity to praise God always have indeed been blessed, and have perhaps contributed more to the peace and happiness of mankind that they had ever previously been able to do with all their ceaseless activity.

14 Facing sickness and death

I

SMELLS and scents evoke memories which help us to recall places and people long since forgotten. Sometimes the memories are difficult to disentangle, and whilst we seek to identify them they can tantalize us like an allusion we cannot quite remember. Sometimes they are brutally obvious, like the smells we associated with our school days when every class-room, corridor, lab, and changing room, refectory, chapel, and even the central stairway, had their own unmistakable aroma. After the holidays, on our return to school, we would sniff disdainfully, like young puppies, and immediately feel comforted and at home; and if we returned in later life we would go through the same process with something akin to affection. We were disappointed if the old familiar smells had gone.

But when we visited the library we could be almost certain that the smells would be the same. With time everything changes, and books today have taken on such a crispness and cleanliness that they would not disgrace a modern hygienic surgery. But libraries inevitably include the old as well as the new, and the smell of musty old books cannot be altered. Jansenius, in the seventeenth century, was said to have died from their musty aroma, and many others since his day have sneezed, or found that smell acted as a strong purgative, whilst others have been bewitched and carried off as not unwilling slaves into fairyland.

Old books, like the shingle on the sea-shore, are obviously full of treasure waiting to be discovered, if only we can be patient and search a little longer. But that is seldom easy. Left alone, surrounded by musty old tomes, I find myself distraught with indecision. Each book, like each new shell a child picks up as he skips along the sands, is something very special. The frontispiece, the cover, the date and title and the curious print, the binding, the feel of the thick paper, the place where it was printed, and the way the type is set are all important. An old book, like a new car, is full of unexpected and enticing assets. Only the smell persists unchanged.

Sometimes the external wrappings so beguile us that we can do no more than examine the book with care and marvel at the craftsmen who produced such beauty. We need to be strong-minded if we are to sit down and read. Within a library filled with such treasures the opportunities are endless, and it is difficult to commit oneself. Hesitantly we have all made our little piles of selected volumes, and noted the titles of other books we do not want to miss. We think we have all the time in the world, as we plan for the future and decide which windows we should open on a new and exciting unexplored world.

But time moves on whatever we may do, and one day we find that time is running out on us and we are now faced with a different situation. The world no longer lies at our young feet, and the library of life with the endless opportunities it offers is closed and out of reach. It is as if we were suddenly transported to a prison where we hear the steel doors slamming and the noisy locks turning in one door after yet another, whilst the footsteps of the gaoler recede into the background behind more locked doors than we can safely count as their dying echoes reverberate around us. We ere left alone, imprisoned in our own cell where we can only hear the sound of our own breathing. We had been surrounded by life and activity and endless opportunities, and now nothing apparently is left.

The books we had hoped to read snap shut, and we have lost our Aladdin's lamp which once opened the doors to new worlds of mystery and delight. Uncertain, in a new situation which we have never before experienced, we recall the libraries we have known, and all those inaccessible well-stocked shelves we had hoped to master. We know now that that day will never dawn—at least on earth. The future we had thought to control has disappeared like the echoing footsteps of the departing gaoler. Alone, we are cut off from those aromas which evoke the past, and from all of those accustomed places and faces which we knew so well. Gradually, sometimes only with great effort, do those facing death transfer their attention to the new world, the new challenge which is now facing them; and then you can almost see them beginning to relax so far as the worries and uncertainties of this life are concerned. There are new and more important worlds opening up before them.

Most of the chapters of their own personal lives have now been written, and they can see their life, like a book almost completed, being slowly closed and put high up upon a shelf. They want to cry out to the reader that there are still important chapters to be written, that the best is yet to come; but they know they cry in vain. The end, they feel, is inevitable, and they can see it drawing near. Often, of course, they are mistaken in their reading of the signs and indications of their own imminent demise, and sometimes there are many valuable chapters still waiting to be written before the book of their life will be finally closed. I have known several men who have repeatedly apologized for taking much longer to die than they had at first suspected.

Another man I knew retired to his bed at the age of sixty-eight to die, and was given two years at the most to live. He had a bad heart, and became a complete invalid. At that time I was leaving to join the Jesuit novitiate, and we said good-bye, as we did not expect to meet again. After two years in bed he recovered his strength, and got so much better that by the time I returned some five years later he was up and about, reading and writing and walking to his club and the local library every day, and in between whiles pottering in the garden. He died nearly twenty years later in his late eighties, very happy and contented. He was blessed with a wonderful wife, and but for her efforts he would probably have died in his late sixties. She strengthened his faith, and gave him new hope despite the certainty of death. Once he had faced death he was less afraid.

Today few people dare to speak of death. It is seen as the ultimate disaster. We are even shielded from thinking about it. We leave to others the care for our dying loved ones, and, once they are dead, we leave to others the arrangements concerning the funeral and burial. Under the guise of not allowing the close relatives to be bothered, we remove from the bereaved those very natural things which would distract them, and prevent them from feeding on their sorrow.

This change, which I think is in many ways a change for the worse, has taken place only in our own lifetime. There was a day, not long ago, when everyone saw death in the course of their normal life. Many children died when young. The elderly usually died where they had lived, and, whether you liked it or not, you could not easily avoid coming in close contact with the dead in your own home. Today improved medical facilities have certainly helped those who need more expert nursing, but an unfortunate result of the end of long-established customs has been that it is now far easier than it ever used to be to ignore death, and even to avoid all contact with and thought about it.

Once death ceases to be that harsh reality which we inevitably meet in others, our imagination takes over. Fantasies, more frightening than the reality, replace sombre facts.

The many old priests and brothers who used to live and die

within religious communities were an inspiration to the
young. Not because they were heroes, or courageous, but
because of what they taught by their lives. They were normal,
sensible men who had one foot firmly in this world and would
go on fighting for their lives to the last moment, and one foot
firmly in heaven so that they could put their trust in God.

They would have laughed at the idea that, because
evolutionary ideas explain so much, we should expect immediate signs of spiritual growth in our own lives when we are
dying; that spiralling upwards is the norm. Admittedly St.
John of the Cross and many spiritual writers have stressed
ascent in the way of perfection. The modern Church stresses
rather the concept of the pilgrim, and, like St. Augustine,
urges us to think of ourselves as 'resident aliens'—responsible
for the world around us because we are residents; but 'aliens'
because our home is in heaven.

Our Lord pointed to this truth when he said 'render unto
Caesar the things that are Caesar's, and unto God the things
that are God's'. If we put it the other way round it seems to
emphasize the truth that unless we fulfil our responsibilities in
the world we shall not be the sort of people who can fulfil their
responsibilities to God, and of course vice versa; if we fail in
our responsibilities to God we shall have made ourselves
incapable of fulfilling our responsibilities in and to the world.
Christ held up the one coin, with the two sides, as if to
emphasize that a fault on one side inevitably led to fault on the
other. We have to be rounded people, prepared to face the
world as well as God.

I well remember one man who was afraid of death. He went
to Lourdes, and the fear left him. Subsequently he often discussed what would happen when he died: would he choke
and gasp—or what? He was no longer afraid, but just wanted
to know. I reassured him that very many people thought death
came like falling asleep. That is what happened to him. One
night, when a sister was watching him as he lay asleep, his
chest stopped rising, and he had gone. There was not even a
sigh to note his passing. He did not think that he had lived a

particularly holy life—though he had certainly tried. But when he knew death was inevitable and imminent his trust in the mercy of God grew, and his fears disappeared. I have known the same thing happen with so many other people—a young girl, a middle-aged and married postman, the mother of a family of ten, and many elderly people—that I do not think it is so unusual.

Many old brothers and priests had a wry sense of humour about death. They knew it was a mistake to take life too seriously, and in their piquant, whimsical way they enjoyed even their last illness. One used to enjoy getting into bed without taking off his boots and, when the Infirmarian remonstrated, replied he would like it to be said that he died with his boots on. My friend who went to Lourdes used to make outrageous jokes which shocked the medical staff, who were not used to death being treated so lightly. Another I remember died content when hearing that Freddie Trueman had shattered the Australians; for another it was Chelsea's position in the Football League which cheered him as he lay seriously ill. They all had their own special interests, as well as liking their pint or snuff, or in many cases a filthy old pipe. They were very normal.

For such people death is not a tragedy, it is a part of the journey to be accepted like the rest of God's good gifts. Unless we meet such people, how can we hope to see death in perspective? The priest is fortunate, for he meets many such people who share the same attitude as those old priests and brothers; but that is not the attitude of the secular world. When those with a Christian faith shun death as a subject to be avoided, instead of bringing a sensible, balanced outlook into the world around them they too often allow the values of that world to infiltrate their own.

II

This is not, of course, to deny that death can bring unspeakable grief and a sense of loss to those who are left behind—especially when it is a child or a younger person who dies. My own experience has been that the children and young people themselves, with a little encouragement, can fairly easily accept the situation. Very often they are not afraid of death when they are called upon to face it. They like things to be black and white, and should not be deceived. It is the parents who really suffer on these occasions.

But many are, and still more think they will be, afraid of death, and cannot go to Lourdes like my good friend. How can they be helped? I remember a young boy of fourteen who was not a Catholic, and so far as I can remember had no religious faith. His father died, and he was terrified lest his mother should also be taken from him. He was obsessed by the thought of death, by fear of death, and could see no further. To such as he, an insight into what Christians believe about the purpose of life and of Christ's resurrection from the dead comes as a blinding revelation. 'Too good to be true'—'surely a fantasy woven by men to delude those momentarily off balance'—yet as Christians we know that our faith provides us with intelligible answers. Why, then, are we so often afraid to share our faith with others who are in need? Perhaps if we did it might help us to overcome our fears, and stir up our own faith in the infinite mercy and love of God our Father about which Our Lord tried to teach us. Too often, because we have ourselves been over-protected from meeting death, our imaginations are stronger than our faith.

From what I have seen in hospital, when death comes to a patient, usually in the early hours of the morning, the screens are placed round the bed. The chaplain will be there if he can. The nurses are busy. The relatives cannot spend all night waiting, night after night. The dying person is lucky if he does not die alone. At such moments he may welcome someone to hold his hand. At least he ought, if possible, to have been prepared.

Many hospital chaplains find that it is the sorrowing parents and relatives, and not the dying, who take up most of their time. But it is the dying who should first be helped. Sometimes the dying do not appreciate how ill they are, and it is always a delicate matter, in conjunction with the doctors, nurses, and relatives, to decide who should tell them and when this should be done. With only a very limited experience I often found that people had to be prepared over several days, so that when they were finally told that death was imminent they could accept the situation. To help those who have no faith is infinitely harder, and calls for more experience than I can muster.

Before the war, when I was at Heythrop in the countryside near Oxford, I remember the Rector, a wise and kindly old man as I then thought, though on reflection now I realize he was only in his early fifties, remarking that it was important to have a number of old and sick and dying in the house, as it brought down 'the blessing of God' on the place. At the time I thought this was just another pious platitude, the sort of remark one expected from a religious superior, a way of rationalizing a difficulty. It is always comfortable to feel that God is on your side. Only in later life did I realize how true his statement was.

Obviously we cannot prove that 'the old bring down the blessing of God upon a house', and, like so many other pious assertions, this too can be easily put in the waste-paper box without more ado. Upon reflection this would, I think, be a serious mistake. As with many of the truths of life, its veracity can only be established from experience or observation—and both would seem to support it.

This is not to try to argue that the old and sick are saints. They are often stubborn and difficult, quarrelsome and cantankerous, frustrated, fretful and sometimes suffering personality and identity crises as a result of drugs. They often drain our mental and psychic nervous energy. But despite all that can be said against them—and sometimes volumes could be written—once they have accepted and come to terms with their illness or the immediacy of death, they have a message for mankind which all men need to know, and which comes

over strongly to those who try to help them. When they are
gone we find that it is not only as friends that we miss them.
We miss them above all as spiritual guides.

On a deeper level also this is true. Whenever we give
because we love, we always receive more than we give. This is
the story of human life, that growth comes by giving. Our Lord
so often pointed it out to his disciples:

> Unless a grain of wheat falls into the earth
>   and dies,
> it remains alone;
> but if it dies,
> it bears much fruit.

This is the story we see enacted before our eyes by all the
seasons of the year; it is the story too which the old and dying
have to try to grasp and to live out in their lives and deaths; and
we, by our caring for and our association with them, are
privileged not only to learn the message with our minds but to
allow that truth to enter our own lives and hearts. It is we who
benefit the most if and when we are privileged to look after the
dying.

III

What then should we say to the old and sick? They help us, but
how can we help them? What is their greatest need, apart from
health, once they have come to terms with the reality of death?

They are very human, and quite simply their greatest need
is, I think, to be loved and appreciated for themselves, for
what they are and for what they are doing, and not just for
what they have done.

They will usually talk at great length about their deeds; they
will talk about glories now forgotten and unknown; they will
fight again their old campaigns. That is natural enough. We all
do it, even those of us who are not very old or very sick. We
forget our failures, and remember the highlights of our lives,

so that we may encourage ourselves to face the present. That is precisely what the old are doing. They know they need encouragement. Our memories are curiously selective. Past sorrows and failures, grievous though they were at the time, fade into the background and, like shadowy figures in an old painting, tone down, until they are almost lost to sight; our achievements take on a sharper brilliance all their own, and so dominate our horizons of the past that we think all must see them. It is as if nature herself would encourage us to forget the past, except in so far as it may spur us on to face what is ahead. Solzhenitsyn's principle of the 'last inch' applies above all for the dying. Without that last inch of effort the material for a wedding dress or a shroud is wasted, the masterpiece ruined without that inch which provides the necessary background, the car unpolished, the crockery dirty. In all things we must finish the job, and it is the last inch that in the final reckoning is the most important of all. The old and sick labour the past so that we may follow the road they trod so long ago, and catch up with them in the present. Too often we stay in the past to which they point and fail to take the hint, and help them here and now when they need appreciation and encouragement.

Hopkins once said: 'The finest pleasure is not to do a thing, but to feel that you could, and the mortification that goes to the heart is to feel it is the power that fails you. . . . It kills me to be time's eunuch and never to beget.' But that is precisely what at first sight faces the old. No wonder so often they turn their face to the wall and lose the will to live. What have they got to live for? If they and we can see it aright, there is much to be done and we can help each other.

If we believe in the mystical body of Christ and the strength of the Spirit, then the reality is full of hope, and a far cry from despair.

> I am the vine,
> you are the branches.
> Whoever remains in me, with me in him,
> bears fruit in plenty.

So often we get things hopelessly wrong, mesmerized by the physical world around us. Buildings are looked upon as achievements—whether they are our private homes, churches or schools. We see success in the laying out of gardens, new health or youth centres, new organizations, research, books. We only need to look in at any archaeological dig to see the transience of bricks and mortar and bank balances. Pushing back the boundaries of ignorance and prejudice, adding to the sum of human wisdom will be more lasting than any physical imprints we may make upon the sands of time; they are necessary and worth while. But is that how, in the final analysis, we should estimate success? We tend to be myopic and, with our horizons foreshortened, see success within our grasp. It is, but in a dimension different from that of this physical and intellectual world around us.

For success to last for ever it has to have a quality of the infinite within it. 'As you did it to one of the least of these my brethren, you did it to me', 'a cup of water given in my name'. Those impulses which motivated a Martin of Tours or a St. Edward the Confessor to follow the paths of generous charity which we traditionally associate with St. Christopher and St. George are now part of them in heaven. It is of such actions that the texture of happiness on earth and in heaven is woven. The seamless robe of the mystical Christ, stretching out to the furthermost corners of the world, and going backwards and forwards in history to the end of time, wraps Christ's brothers for all eternity in the infinite happiness of heaven; but it is woven here and now by all who seek to spread Christ's Kingdom in the hearts of men, and it is woven for all eternity and never will be lost. That is the task the old and sick can do. They do it more effectively than we who, distracted by the 'trifles light as air', the froth and bubbles, baubles, trinkets, trivia—call them what you will—waste our lives on the ephemeral. That is why the dying can be such effective spiritual guides.

I am convinced that when the final reckoning is made we shall be aghast at the folly and incredible stupidity of selfish men who thought old age or sickness was a waste of time.

What is time for? That is the question, and if we get that wrong, then no wonder we destroy things of infinite worth, or at least fail to appreciate them for what they are. Mgr. Ronald Knox, I seem to remember, remarked how extreme old age and serious sickness wonderfully free the spirit. At last, we are told, we can see things as they are and get our values true. At last we are becoming free. We can opt out. No wonder the very old and very sick want to be appreciated for the balanced views and insights which they have, and also, quite rightly, for what they are doing with their lives in their final suffering. Because of their physical infirmities, because they are so closely identified with Christ on his cross, because their hands and feet are tied and their lips too swollen to speak easily, they are entering into the Passion of Christ in a way denied to lesser men. 'Come down from the Cross', Christ's enemies jeered. Woe betide us if we say something not dissimilar to the friends of Christ who are suffering with and for him, and are building up the Kingdom of Christ on earth as well as in heaven. Because the hearts of the old and very sick are in heaven, only those utterly blind to all spiritual and human values can have the folly even to think they are no earthly good.

Our Lady stood at the feet of Christ's cross. Somehow she found it in her heart, so Catholic tradition has always believed, to encourage Christ on his cross. Surely that is what we are called to do for the sick and very old. Their hearts may be in heaven but they are very human and, like us, welcome the encouragement of their friends.

I knew one wonderful nurse who I think has helped countless priests into heaven—and priests even more than most need to be helped in their last agony and encouraged to pray—by saying with them short prayers they knew: the Angelus, the rosary in short bursts, and other prayers at regular intervals all through the day and night. It all looked so very simple until one had to try to do it oneself, and then one found how utterly incompetent and unqualified one was to talk of the deepest things of God to a man or woman about to cross the threshold. But incompetence is no excuse. Just as the actor may fear he will be overcome with stage fright on a first night, and has to face his fears and incorporate his tensions into his acting so that his personality takes on a new quality—so, too, when we feel ourselves, and know ourselves, incompetent and inadequate for the task, we have to accept that unpalatable truth, digest it quickly, and by recognizing our weakness acquire a strength, a quality, maybe an openness we would never otherwise have possessed. All things work together for good, if only we can see them aright, and use them too.

IV

And that is precisely what the sick and the very old are doing, or want to do, and what we should be encouraging them to do. That is all very well, I can hear my friends say, when you are speaking of old priests or nuns, or people of a strong faith. But what do you say to a young mother who dare not die and leave her children unprotected, or to a woman who knows her husband desperately needs her, or to a child who has no faith? What do you say, when indeed the death is so clearly a major tragedy for those who are left behind, and the sick person knows this? However willingly, or at least patiently, they may have accepted suffering in this world, they cannot easily bear to be the cause of further distress to those most dear to them. If indeed they have a spark of Christian faith one can point out to them that their lot is not unlike that which faced Christ. He had come to do a job of work for the world. He knew his Apostles had not yet fully grasped his message; that humanly speaking his work was not half done; that he could not afford to leave the Apostles alone; that he needed a miracle so that he could have more time; that if ever a man was indispensable then it was he himself, when he was only just beginning to come to the height of his physical and mental powers. He had come to save the world. The physical death he died on the cross must have been much easier to accept than the apparent sacrifice of all his hopes for all his loved ones. The frustration, the failure, the hopelessness for the future—these must have appalled him. He must have hoped that if he died no others would need to suffer. But they would, and his sufferings would give to theirs a positive value which otherwise they could never have had. He had to suffer it all, first.

The Christian can try to enter into the mind of Christ and accept the personal and spiritual crosses no less than the physical ones which come his way. He can, and must, try to do more. He should see all things as the gifts of God, and this includes all crosses and trials, triumphs and disappointments, good health and bad health, a short life apparently ruined by the crass stupidity or wickedness of others, a long life crippled by disease. With faith we can see them as the gifts of God; and gifts are not meant to be accepted with a grudging spirit.

His gifts are for our good, to help us grow, once pruned, to a fullness of life otherwise impossible. The capacity of the thimble, the tumbler, the bucket or the bath can only be increased if the old frame is radically altered. With reflection most of us can see how we have often foolishly complained about what we can now see, with hindsight, were the gifts of an infinitely wise and loving God who ignored our tremulous and childish wailings. It has happened so often. In times of great physical, mental, or spiritual distress, the sick and the very old need to be encouraged to accept their pain and suffering as the gift of God: something precious; something which can open to them, even in their extreme old age, new worlds of which we have not dreamt. The trouble really is that we, who should be helping them, are so limited in our own little world, so incapable of realizing something of the grandeur and greatness of the opportunities which are being offered to those we love, and who we are very conscious are suffering intensely, that we tend to play the devil's advocate. To accept is one thing, but gifts are to be loved; and, whether we like them or would prefer to be without them, we have to try to see them for what they are: gifts God has specially selected for our own particular needs. Under the grace of God we can grow in a second. As the Curé d'Ars said, between jumping off the bridge and hitting the water we can grow into the likeness of Christ. Who are we, with our eyes in blinkers, to put limits and bounds to what Christ wants for his friends—the old and the sick?

V

But what can one say to the man who does not know Christ and does not believe in the things of the spirit; to the man who would rail against God and his painful lot like the thief of the cross who refused to turn to Christ, to the man overcome with a sense of guilt who thinks a cruel God is punishing him for his many crimes? How can one help such a man? He is following his own way of the cross by which one can be certain God wants to lead him to his own beloved son on his cross. Whatever there is of faith, or hope, or charity, these are the sparks which must be fanned. Love for his wife or daughter or grandchildren; concern for his overworked nurse; patience in pain; gratitude for little kindnesses; all these, and much else besides, may indicate that he is an anonymous Christian, denying Christ in the name of Christ, denying God in the name of God, because he has got the names mixed up. He needs right thoughts of God. So often, underneath, one finds that the real values which animate the apparent atheist are, unknown to him, values he has acquired from our common Christian heritage. Scratch him deeply, and you find the faith. Sometimes, alas, this may not appear to be so; but who are we to pit our minds against the wisdom of God, or to limit his love and mercy to what we can comprehend?

The fault, too often, for the tragic plight of the non-Christian is our failure, the failure of Christians everywhere, to show by the quality of our lives the true values which animate us. Newman said, 'The Gospel is . . . not a philosophy . . . nor a mere quality of mind . . . nor a sentiment or subjective opinion but a substantive message from above, guarded and preserved in a visible polity.' Too often we substitute civilization and culture for religion and, like the old nineteenth-century liberals, seek to bring all things under the banner of reason. Once we lose sight of the place which mysteries should play in our lives, we have to put our trust in the academic experts—and who can blame the anonymous Christian for doubting their capacity to lead?

The function of the old and sick is to help us keep our values balanced, and from time to time give us a glimpse of that heavenly Kingdom to which, like the Israelites in the wilderness, God's providence would lead us. We can pray with Cardinal Newman, in his prayer:

> Lead, Kindly Light, amid the encircling gloom
> Lead thou me on!
> The night is dark, and I am far from home—
> Lead thou me on!
> Keep thou my feet; I do not ask to see
> The distant scene—one step enough for me.

15 Thoughts on heaven

I

WE can think of death as an end to suffering and pain; as
goodbye to our hopes and goodbye to our friends; as the end of
the beginning and the passing over into a new life.

I always think of an old-fashioned crowded railway station
which still retains some of the smells and smoke from the
recent past. Everything is bustle and confusion as passengers
stumble over the piles of luggage, dash between the trolleys
laden high with sacks of mail. They push and pull their way
with all their clobber on to the train. They force their way with
stern determination through the hordes of those descending.
There is no time to be lost. Soon, too soon for some, the doors
begin to slam, and, as the chaos subsides, there is an ever
heightening sense of expectation. Just as in the crowded foyer
of a theatre on a first night, when the insistent bell urges the
audience to resume their seats, so on the platform there is a
final moment of suspense, suddenly pierced by the shrill notes

of the whistle. As the train gathers speed and the last farewells are said, frantic parents and dear frail old ladies try to keep pace, and are left behind. The all-important final messages and directions are wafted away on the unsubstantial air where none can hear them and, whilst handkerchiefs flutter and arms and paper wave, the dear one departs in peace and tranquillity to his destination.

As we pull the sheets over the face of a dear friend, the chaos and confusion, the shouting and the last messages, the cries and tears and grief are all our own. Our dear one has gone off upon a journey. Just as the friend we saw off at the station is often already settling himself comfortably into his seat, and lighting his pipe as he looks out of the window, or is trying to open his paper at the page he wants to read, whilst we, left on the platform, are still recovering our bits and pieces and lost children and all the other things with which the seeing off of friends always seem to be lumbered. He, serene, blissfully unaware of all the fuss and bother, goes on his way in peace.

It is we, not he, who are disturbed. Our departed friend is not unlike the driver who quietly and contentedly drives along a road where the majority of drivers are impatient and mostly break the law. He urges his aged vehicle along, with his cap half over his eyes, serenely unaware of the sudden squeaks and brakings, the hootings and bumpings and sounds of tinkling glass, as far from godly language disturbs the ever-lengthening queue of cars behind him. You cannot really blame him. If others want to drive themselves to distraction, what can he do about it? His ancient car can do no more.

Nor can we blame our dear departed friends for the grief and sorrow they cause us by their leaving. Christ wept for Lazarus, and shared the grief of Martha and Mary. Our sorrow is very real; we need our friends and miss them when they go. But all the same, I wonder if we don't take death too seriously, as though it were the end of everything. Are we upset because our own lives have to be rearranged? Our grief can be a very selfish thing.

Death is obviously a major crossroads: for those who believe in Christ more of a reunion than a parting, however painful that parting may be for those of us who are left behind. We think of our friend as starting on a journey and leaving us behind. How does he view it? Death is the climax of his life, which makes intelligible all that went before. This, we hope, is his moment of triumph when he enters into glory. The Apostles saw Our Lord ascend into heaven, and they went home with joy. At last they understood that this was his moment of triumph.

II

St. Leo speaks of the Apostles, after Our Lord ascended into heaven, unexpectedly discovering, whilst they were still suffering from the shock of loss, that they had found him in a new way. Though they could no longer see him in his humanity, he was closer to them in his godhead than they had previously experienced. Because of this new mysterious presence of the Lord, the Apostles went home with joy. They knew the promises Christ had made—that he would not leave them orphans, that he would be with them forever—were being fulfilled. His triumph and his new presence were not unconnected.

Like the Apostles before the Ascension of Our Lord, we tend to think that the physical presence of our friends is all-important, as though our relationships were limited to sight and touch. We easily forget that, important though touch and sight may be, they do not create the heart of the relationship. When our friends die, we all experience something similar to what the Apostles felt when they lost and found Our Lord after his Ascension. Stricken with grief at our loss, we experience a new, deeper, even warmer, certainly more mysterious relationship, which defies explanation. At first sight we tend to dismiss this as emotional; as something similar to the pain which severed nerve-ends cause in the foot after the leg has long since been amputated. I do not profess to know the answer, but I don't see whey we should be surprised, since we believe in the Resurrection. Our Lord promised:

> If anyone believes in me, even though he dies he will live,
> and whoever lives and believes in me
> will never die.

We believe in our on-going relationship with the Risen Christ so that, as St. Paul says: 'if we live, we live for the Lord; and if we die, we die for the Lord, so that alive or dead we belong to the Lord. This explains why Christ both died and came to life, it was so that he might be Lord both of the dead and of the living.' We recognize him as Lord of all. We believe too in our friendship with one another 'in the Lord'.

Our friendships are more than emotional. We can speak of them as spiritual, or mystical, or at any rate as deeper and more lasting than a mere sense perception. Our relationships with the Risen Christ, and with him and through him with one another, are rooted in the deepest parts of our own being. When we express our faith in the Resurrection of Christ, we express our faith in a truth which affects all our human relationships too. No wonder this truth, which is at the heart of our faith, affects every part of our daily lives.

Our Lord's insistence that

> I am going now to prepare a place for you
> and after I have gone and prepared you a place,
> I shall return to take you with me;
> so that where I am
> you may be too

should help to take away our fears, not only for ourselves but for our loved ones, and provide us with confidence for our continuing relationships with them in and through Christ.

As he lay dying at the age of 45, Gerard Manley Hopkins kept on exclaiming: 'I am so happy, I am so happy.'

Yet the fact remains that we are still conscious of our sins and faults and failings, and know that our dear friends were not without them too. In these circumstances we need always to remember that he who tries to comfort us is both God and Man; he has no illusions about us, and still loves us, as he has proved in countless ways. To doubt his power or willingness to forgive may well be a sin we would not commit if we would only listen to his words.

So I wonder sometimes if we Christians don't rather overdo our fear of death, and underestimate Our Lord's words, which, if they are to mean anything at all, must, as St. Paul so clearly thought, be taken at their face value; as meaning precisely what they say. Why else should he have written to the Colossians: 'Let your thoughts be on heavenly things, not on the things that are on the earth, because you have died, and now the life you have is hidden with Christ in God. But when Christ is revealed—and he is your life—you too will be revealed in all your glory with him.'

Admittedly it still remains true that nothing defiled can enter Heaven, that all have sinned and need the forgiveness of God, that after death the Judgement; that Purgatory and Hell are part of our Faith. He has to tell us this perhaps because, unless we are shown the whole canvas, we cannot begin to grasp the infinite mercy and love of a God who does not want the death of the sinner but that he may have life, and have it more abundantly.

III

Whatever psychiatrists and philosophers may say about the body–soul relationship, all I think would agree that externals can be deceptive. A beautiful face or a beautiful body does not guarantee an attractive personality, and the obverse is equally true. Yet the disparity never ceases to surprise. The faces of the elderly, and their voices too, often reveal what was hidden when they were young, but it would still seem to be axiomatic that the externals conceal more than they reveal of the true human personality.

I wonder if in heaven the relationship is reversed, so that the glorified body's main function is to witness to the unique characteristics and personality of a unique person. This could explain why the children at Fatima and St. Bernadette at Lourdes could not give an easily intelligible picture of the beautiful lady. All her qualities, all her goodness were no longer hidden, but shown forth as her identifying characteristics.

This could also explain why the Apostles and the Disciples failed at first to recognize Our Lord in his glorified body until his actions revealed him as the Risen Lord. Then they recognized his qualities, and so were able to see he was the same but different.

If this conjecture were to have any truth within it, then it would seem that heaven should be thought of not so much as a place of rest, as of perpetual and never-ending growth, where our whole being will be absorbed in giving ever more, and receiving ever more, of the infinite inexhaustible love of God himself.

> What no eye has seen, nor ear heard,
> nor the heart of man conceived,
> what God has prepared for those who love him.

Why do we insist on putting limits to his love? I suppose we are always afraid of being disappointed, and hedge our bets. We hope that by playing down the joys of heaven we may, in the end, be pleasurably surprised. Often heaven seems rather a chancy business, so we concentrate on the present and forget St. Paul's injunction: 'If then you have been raised with Christ, seek the things that are above, where Christ is, seated at the right hand of God.'

St. Paul was only making explicit what Christ had always taught: that we should be encouraged by the thought of heaven. Unashamedly Christ put before us the things he knew we love and appreciate: a wedding feast, a marriage, a bride and bridegroom, a banquet. He did not seek to win us with pious unworldly thoughts, a philosophy of life, or even an

academic meeting of old friends where thoughts and time
would fly.

Here we only get the faintest glimmerings, the most fleeting
of insights, but they are surely given so that we may be strengthened and encouraged. It is not too good to be true. It is true.

IV

Happy the man who thinks of heaven as home, and home as
heaven. The love of a mother, the care of a father, the most
tender, the strongest and the most enduring of childhood
memories are, in later life, seen as more than mere memories
of a loved and bygone age, they are seen as insights into
hidden truths granted to the very young, and then more
slowly, gradually, unveiled throughout our lifetimes. Those
insights are doubly real. They are and were some of our earliest experiences which will be with us for ever, and they point
to a hidden truth of which they were but a hint, a whisper: the
Fatherhood of God, and the love of Christ's own Mother
whom he gave us as our own when he said to his mother:
'Woman, behold, your son!' and to his disciple, 'Behold, your
mother!'

In the love of every human family we can see glimpses of
heaven, and slowly understand that there is a harmony and
fitness about all things, so that even the created physical
world, and still more man, redeemed by Christ, seek, as im-
pelled and drawn by the Spirit, to fit into that delicate jigsaw
where all things shall be in harmony and all reveal the wonders of his love.

St. Paul saw the whole of creation 'groaning in one great act
of giving birth; and not only creation, but all of us who possess
the first-fruits of the Spirit, we too groan inwardly as we wait
for our bodies to be set free'. The orchestrated song of the
curlews and the storms at sea and man in many moods; the
sweet smells of the early spring and the dankness of decaying
vegetation in the woods in the autumn; the highlights and the

sombre moments of a lifetime, like all the many colours of a man-made picture, must in God's masterpiece all fit together, and we shall be at home.

All the past, then, takes on new meaning, and the whispers and the hints and the secret tuggings at the heart, which urged us on almost unnoticed, will begin to be understood. All that, it seems to me, should never be thought of as static, but vibrant with life and lasting for ever. God's plan to give himself to man can never have an end. Eternity is needed.

Our home on earth is meant to be a foretaste, a preparation, where we can so be nurtured that we carry our heaven with us all through our lives; like the buds not yet fully open. The burgeoning is to be in heaven, where we shall find that dream of the happiness of the perfect home which we have ever carried in our hearts is indeed our home, writ large, with a new dimension of wonder, love and energetic happiness.

No wonder our departed friends are anxious to be upon their way; but sometimes it may be that they are not yet ready, and would not feel at home in the heaven for which our lives on earth had been meant to be this foretaste and preparation. As Catholics we believe that God in his goodness and love for man may sometimes give us further preparation in Purgatory, and that, just as we can and should help our friends on earth, so can we pray for our loved ones who have died that they may be finally fitted out, as it were, if aught is missing. Such prayers, of course, like all prayers, serve a double purpose. They may indeed help our friends, should they need help and should God so dispose. They also are helpful to ourselves. They remind us of the holiness of God and our own unworthiness and need of his forgiveness all through our lives. But the past must not distract us from the immediacy of our present tasks; it should be a spur to urge us forward to use our present 'now' so well that all things may indeed now, and for all eternity, 'work together for good to them that love God'.

16   You and the Church

I

DEPRESSION, as I have tried to indicate, is the common lot of man. Within the Catholic Church at the present time, this seems to be such a widespread problem as to merit special treatment. Whether it is equally widespread in other Churches I am not able to assess. The two disciples going to Emmaus, as recorded in St. Luke's Gospel, were depressed. 'We had hoped . . .', they complained, and only gradually understood that they were 'slow and foolish of heart'. They had lost heart because they had mistaken success for failure. Once they understood this simple truth their depression vanished; their lives were transformed. Our prejudices are embedded deep in our emotions, and logic alone is not sufficient to remove them.

A salmon spawned high up a mountain stream must experience a sense of shock to its system when, quietly swimming downstream through the placid waters it has always known, it finds itself suddenly being swept along over jagged rocks and falling into deep ice-cold pools far below. The maelstrom of seething, boiling water beneath the cascade slowly eddies forth, and the fish finds itself continuing on its way once again through quiet and placid waters.

The mountain stream forever changing and yet ever the same, now clearly visible, now half-hidden by tangled weeds, the source of life not only for tiny fish and plants and birds and all manner of living things, fed from so many sources and yet feeding others, is in many ways so like Christ's Church. If dammed, it dies, and becomes a dank pond which only breeds disease and death to all who taste it. But if allowed—and perhaps helped to go upon its way, it brings delight and life to all who know it.

When we reflect on the recent years of rapid change within the Catholic Church, no wonder those who from infancy had been prepared to resist all change were disconcerted. It would be pointless to try to weigh the good and bad, the loss and gain in all the many changes which have affected our traditional way of life. We can be sure that for many years to come these years of crises will be meticulously sifted by social and by Church historians, and that many boys and girls at school will inevitably be expected to expound on the aftermath of Vatican II. We can almost read the questions: 'Was the Council a good thing?'—maybe too bald a question, this—but they are sure to be asked to 'compare and contrast', or to 'weigh the loss and gain' to the members of that Church, and to society at large. One can think of many suitable questions calculated to unmask those who have not done their homework.

Underlying all the actual changes in the liturgy, and the confusion that has arisen over the understanding of many doctrines concerning faith and morals which dig deeply into our own personal lives, there has emerged a new attitude. Questions are now asked, where traditionally only answers were expected; and the roles of priests and nuns and the laity have all been subtly altered. For many the new mental attitude is where the problem lies.

We used to bracket the parish priest with the general practitioner. They were trusted, and regarded with affection;

sometimes seen as the unqualified amateurs who had learnt wisdom through the varied experiences of life and could, if necessary, direct one to the experts. The priest with his back to his people represented them before God, and because he did this in the name of Christ, as the *alter Christus*, all personal intonations, gestures, and mannerisms were quite out of place.

It used to be not uncommon for a man who had had a quarrel with a priest to draw a distinction between the man and his priesthood. 'Of course, as a priest I respect you, but . . .' and then the home truths would flow.

The modern priest is more often expected to be a specialist and a theologian, who can not only represent his people, but also enter into dialogue with them all, and fashion them into a community; and so become quite as much their representative—should they so wish it—in speaking up to the Bishop and the various Commissions as he is the Bishop's representative in speaking down to his people.

It might be fair to say that all spiritual movement in the Church used to be seen as coming down from the Holy Spirit, through the Holy Father, to the Bishops and so through the priests to the laity. Even Newman long ago pointed out that such a viewpoint was a caricature of the truth as revealed in scripture and tradition; but the emphasis was so heavily weighted that it is only since Vatican II that has there been that unmistakable visible upsurging of the Spirit from below as well as from above. Give and take has always been essential, but, if the Church is to fulfil her role in the world today and give the witness which is needed, she must be well rooted in the world as well as in the Holy Spirit. Looking back, one can appreciate that there were many times in the history of the Church when men so concentrated on their links with, and their fidelity to, their roots that they underestimated the necessity of communicating that truth in intelligible and meaningful terms to those who did not live within the garden enclosed. Christ came for all men. The Church was made for all men, and she cannot hope to fulfil that role if she is deprived of life-giving contacts with the world through her living members. Each man's witness is unique, and all are necessary.

In all these changes nothing essential is lost. The apparently new upsurge of the Spirit from and through the roots does not deny or denigrate the downward flow as being now less necessary. But when the emphasis on one aspect of the truth clouds our vision of the greater truth, then it is necessary for the Church to underline and place new emphasis on what we were neglecting.

We always wanted our priests and people to grow to ever greater maturity through their faith; we used to say 'grace builds on nature' because we wanted everyone to know that all that God made is good, and can be and should be incorporated into his living body; the personal elements so emphasized today were always present; the priest facing the people, united with them, together sharing in Christ's offering and sacrifice and the new life he came to bring, is nothing new. The priest in his uniform was seen as the representative of the Church speaking to man; without his dog-collar he may be better tuned in to listen not only to the needs of the world but also to those insights into the truth which the world offers. Some of that message he needs himself; some he can subsequently transmit upwards to the deanery, or to a suitable Commission, or to his Bishop. So too with the nuns. They do not exist merely to reassure and comfort those of us who have lived in the Church for many years. They also have a fourfold function of their own, vertical and horizontal, speaking and listening to God and their neighbour, and now one, now the other aspect of that vocation has to be stressed.

II

But what are we to say to the man whose life is certainly disrupted because of the disorder in the Church? Good-naturedly he may dislike, but can accept, eyeball to eyeball confession and Communion in the hand; he can appreciate that great mysteries of our faith forever need new formulation. With new knowledge of the mystery of man, both physical and social, and of Old Testament languages, the moral and biblical theologians are hard pushed, and are no longer always able to give a simple answer in a few words which all can understand. Such basic questions as 'is there a natural law?', on which we can base all our other questions and answers, in a question which itself was seldom asked in the old days; a question of philosophy. Time, under the guidance of the Holy Spirit, has given the Church an insight into how best to express those great truths in which human man-made philosophy and God's divine revelation are mixed. With the sudden increased knowledge of both we should not expect instant answers today.

We cannot and should not assume that there should always be a permanent neat and tidy order, as in the garden enclosed, within the Church. The Infinite has continually to break through. This means that not all the truths we need to know can safely and forever be arranged in a fixed hierarchical form. They will always be true, but as we are given more insight into one or another aspect of that truth, there will necessarily be a shift of emphasis within the whole body of truth. Just as our personal lives take on new shapes, and yet we retain our identity—as do the squared meshes when the fisherman's net is pulled this way or that—so with the Church. At some times, like the fisherman's net, it may look as if it is composed of a host of squares; at other times, under strain, the squares take on a more pointed form of the diamond; but the identity is never lost.

Reflecting on our own lives, we know that whatever was good and true in the past has, because it had something of the infinite within it, always been able to be incorporated into our present; and, once it has been accepted, has opened up a new window and given us a new understanding of the world around us. So too the Church is ever growing—and needs to go on growing for all time—in her understanding of the living truth, Christ himself, whose body she is. We see the Church as the extension of Christ in time, as both human and divine, as Christ is Man and God.

Like the mountain stream, the Church can never be viewed alone, in isolation from the living, pulsing world of which she is a part. Not of the world, she certainly is and must be always in it, or we shall misjudge her badly.

For small children a mountain stream has a magic of its own—a magic which persists into old age—so that the sweet smell of the heather, the grandeur of the distant hills, even the cries of the curlews and the larks far overhead, all pass unnoticed. It is the swirling, rippling stream which holds and absorbs the attention of the child. All else is but a backcloth against which it is seen. Some of us remain children all our lives, and do scant justice to the world around us.

But the Church cannot be so dissociated from the world; it cannot be rightly viewed alone; it is a part of a living whole, the child of history. The storm-clouds far away which drench the upper reaches of the mountain ranges bring moisture from far distant seas transported through the heavens. The stream, still less the Church, cannot rightly be understood except in its true setting. The Church is not a remote philosophy of life—ever unchanged and unchanging—but the life of Christ lived out 'in ten thousand places' in the world as it is today.

Whatever is dross will, as it is slowly sifted by the Church, be rejected and cast out. That will take time. Our job is not to anticipate the work of the Holy Spirit, but to answer his call in our own lives. The present is all-important. Only thus can we make our own unique contribution to that Church of which we are living members.

III

But we are still faced with practical problems. A friend of mine told me in the late sixties that when a newly ordained priest had come to supply in his parish he had complained that too many of the parishioners were wasting his time with unnecessary confession. Not surprisingly the number going to confession dropped. Within six months another young priest went to supply at the same parish. He complained that no one was going to confession, and yet most people were going to Holy Communion—clearly, he thought, in mortal sin. What, asked my friend, were the good parishioners to do?

Obviously both young priests were finding their way, and could and should have been helped by those to whom they were speaking so fiercely. They needed help, and instead were criticized. Too easy to misjudge the situation. The Spirit works up and down, to and fro. As on the London Underground, one can find one has misread the signs and is going in the wrong direction. There always have been, and always will be, mistakes and misunderstandings; there will be valid differences of opinion. There will be a need for confrontations and for those creative tensions from which, as I have tried to show elsewhere, true growth can come. The Church has become an increasingly disorderly affair, but within that orchestrated cacophony of voices there is always room for more. We must be true to ourselves; our own views and voices should be expressed, if they are filled with the Spirit, positive, forward-looking and full of joy. Let others do the judging. It is for us to look below the surface, and see there the Church we ever knew and loved. She is still there.

I remember once meeting a holy Bishop who was afraid of the new movements in the Church. He was a pastoral man. He feared lest the faith of his good people should be disturbed or undermined. Quite rightly, he wanted to ensure that none of those committed to his charge should ever be lost. He tended to resist all change, thinking this was safest.

I was reminded of a mother I knew. She appreciated that she had to teach her son to let go of her apron-strings and learn to walk on his own. This was a lesson which would not be learnt in one fell swoop into the unknown, but gradually, bit by bit. Once confidence was gained fears proved groundless, a body of experiences built up, a mature person gradually emerged who, unknown to himself, had been trained to make his own personal assessment of situations as they arose and to take responsibility for what he had decided. Soon, old enough to make mistakes, he could graduate to trying to avoid making the same mistake twice over.

Somehow the Church must train her laity as that good mother prepared her children for the unknowable challenges of life. Few would deny that in the past the Church was over-protective. She did not expect or provide for decision-making from the laity. Simple obedience—or was it conformity?—was expected. The faithful accepted this safe role, and were content to follow where they were led and to leave the decision-making to those who were 'in charge'.

The final decisions must always rest with those who have the final responsibility: the Pope, the Bishops, and the parish priests and the laity within their respective roles. But those decisions should and must be reached only after discussion with all the rest of the Church, who also have their share of responsibility and some share in the decision-making. To ignore the interactions needed between all parts of a living body is not helpful. To deny they are necessary because for many centuries the Church seemed to get on without them is to deny the Church that freedom which every living body requires.

IV

What are we to say to the man who cannot accept change? Helped he must be. Most intractable problems are best resolved by the influence of people, not by their arguments. The more important truths are caught, not taught. One must find or create a situation where the truth, and not the over-sentimentalized memories of the past, with all their nostalgic overtones, is allowed to seep through.

When I was fortunate enough to be living at Campion Hall I remember how I was well placed to invite people who were worried about the new look of the young Jesuits to come and meet them. They were at first worried about the casual dress. I think that without exception the remedy always worked. To their surprise the old, the depressed, and the discouraged found that the young priests, who came from a great variety of different countries, were invariably as warm, as welcoming, and as dedicated to their work and their priesthood as any of the young men of former days. The young today, they found, were not the inconoclastic revolutionaries intent on destroying the Church whom they had feared, but were very normal, open men, with whom it was easy to talk about serious matters. Perhaps it was this openness which above all won their hearts, and it was their hearts and not their heads which needed converting.

I had already learnt this lesson when I was chaplain to the students at Manchester University. The only safe way to overcome most people's prejudices and unfounded fears is to confront them with the reality. Many people are frightened of university students. Certainly they seldom receive a good press. I was appalled on some occasions by the disparity between events which I had witnessed and the reports I subsequently read.

This discrepancy, the seeming failure of the media to report faithfully facts as we know them, is one of the saddest experiences of life. We all know it in our own lives, but we easily forget that the discrepancy is not caused by ill-will, but by the inherent problems which face anyone trying to communicate the experiences of another. We all see things differently. Naturally there must be discrepancies. What is a fact, or what makes it important? Easy questions to ask, but in the actual world in which we live more difficult to answer.

Mutatis mutandis, we can and should say the same of the modern Church as we do of the university students, and not be too easily misled by what we read, which so often ignores the good and concentrates on the trouble-maker because he is 'news'.

But how can the ordinary man meet the modern Church, if

indeed the real fears are about new attitudes, a new way of life, a new sharing of authority and responsibility, a change of balance within the old structures? Again, the only solution which seems likely to be effective is that new bridges be built and two-way communication be established, so that those who feel isolated, afraid, or disapproving may have an opportunity to identify themselves with the Church, forget the 'they' complex and become personally involved.

V

In the past few years there has been unexpected progress. Other theologians have built new bridges with the Anglicans and Methodists and those of other faiths, or of no faith at all. In every deanery there has been an increase of communication between clergy, young and old, and some of the laity. The Parish Councils, the Senate of Priests, the Commissions, are all easily criticized, but cumulatively they have done much to break down the isolation of the depressed.

Yet the problem remains, for every parish priest I meet tells me the same story—there are still very many who are in need of help. If this is indeed the age of the laity, then surely the laity should help, not with arguments and reasonings and logic and ideas which will only increase the work-load of those already committed to the task, but by their lives, through which the magic of the new Church is not taught but caught. Responsibility demands involvement. Advice can too easily be theoretical, academic, and provide us with an illusion that we have helped. Today the Church needs more than that.

The modern Church, as we can not unreasonably call it, is the old Church that we used to know, written in larger letters. It is still the Church for which the martyrs died, the one we thought we knew, the Church which always seemed so impervious to change or argument, and so authoritative too. As children grow up, and yet in their mothers' eyes always remain the same—and who can tell which is the truer vision—so does the Church. We need not be surprised nor fearful when we find in the Church, as in our children, new questions being asked and new reactions which to us seem unexpected. The Church remains unchanging, faithful, though she is changing all the time, for she is living with the Spirit, and is both human and divine. With one foot in the world, she may at times appear over-worldly, too much concerned with social justice and the rights of God's own poor, but she will never cease to bring forth from the treasury God gives her his message for mankind, and that must still be given, by Bishops, priests, and nuns, and the most ordinary of men, prepared for each new occasion as opportunity demands. There can never be an end, on earth, to what the good God gives us, in giving us his Son, and with him and through him too, his spirit to unite us with our Father in one faith, and through Christ his Son with everyone on earth. The victory is won.

> For he has made known to us
> in all wisdom and insight
> the mystery of his will,
> according to his purpose
> which he set forth in Christ
> as a plan for the fulness of time,
> to unite all things in him,
> things in heaven and things on earth.

17   The pub in the world

I dreamt I was in a pub I had known well but which, only six months before, had been badly damaged by fire. Much of the old half-timbered house had been destroyed. A new modern rectangular box with no-nonsense harsh exterior lines replaced what had been lost. It fitted oddly on to the little that remained of the friendly gabled building we had known so well. Inside everything was new. Gone were the cobwebs, the dust of ages and the long hard seats against the wall. New brass knick-knacks shone in all the corners. Only the smell of beer and stale tobacco, much the same as it had ever been, brought back the memories of the past. The crowd was just the same.

There was the young man looking for a worthwhile job, wondering where life would lead him. He had had no vision, but he had no fears. The world, he thought, still lay at his young feet and was his for the taking. The farm labourer who had had a row that morning with his boss was there. He never carried a watch, and was often late for work; that morning there had been what he called a confrontation. The word sounded odd upon his lips. The new-fangled ways were not for the likes of him. If only he was left alone he did a decent job in his own way, which was the only way he knew. Not easily could men like him be pushed around by those who had not heard that time in country places is quite different from what it is in towns.

The long-distance lorry-driver was still without much happiness. His marriage had broken up, and he was indulging in a long fit of depression, as he tortured himself with the thought of what might have been. He had loved his wife, and she loved him too, but it had never worked. He had always taken her for granted, like his favourite chair by the fire, and one day she was there no longer. Tired, she had upped and gone, little realizing that she had not lost her man. Admittedly he had treated her like he treated his lorry, which he drove mercilessly through day and night; yet he had really loved her. He had loved them both.

The elderly man from the garage was there, a decent chap, but difficult to get to know. So too was the former bank manager and his ex-army friend, both compulsorily retired comparatively young; time was heavy on their hands. As usual they discussed the news and put the world to rights. Their gardens and odd jobs about the house filled in their days, but not their hearts or minds. Sometimes they brought the vicar or the visiting Catholic priest in for a drink, as neither would come in on his own. They knew that they were finished, rejects of the world, because their age was against them. That was the way things went, but they felt it was a funny sort of world which treated them so shabbily. Their friends, some even younger, suffered similar fates. There was no point in being bitter, but they exuded little of that *joie de vivre* which, like champagne, can help when things are bad. Their positive contribution was virtually nil. They made, as well as found, the going hard. Then there were the two young lovers, students from the polytechnic, and several others whom I did not know. Only the girl with the long fair hair was missing; her husband had finally left her, and she could not easily get away, as the children came home for midday lunch—it was much better and cheaper than at school.

As usual, the conversation got round to the subject of the new pub. Nobody liked it. It was new. They all preferred the old. As I listened I was fascinated by the arguments, which had little to do with the old pub we had known for many years. Some lived, I thought, in an unreal world, some in a world which none of us had ever known, and some in a world which, like the old pub, had gone for ever; and so, untroubled by the solemnity of solid facts, they were free to let their fancies roam, and roam they did. Was it escapism? It sounded pretty harmless.

Their discontents with the new pub, I ventured to suggest, came not from broken hearts, but from a far less worthy source. They had not been consulted. They had had no hand in initiating the change. Their pride was dented, and their ego had risen in revolt. No wonder they disliked the change—a memorial, as it were, to their insignificance.

In their own humble estimation, they had deserved better treatment. Within their houses they were forever making alterations, and all their changes were of course for the best. Guilty of male chauvinism, they would indeed have been quite shattered had not their wives and friends acclaimed their prowess, and admired what they had so laboriously thought up and done within the garden and the inner sanctum which made up their home. This, after all, was really very natural. What we do ourselves, like our ideas, must obviously be good. We see that very clearly. What others do, especially when it disturbs our normal way of life, so often is unnecessary and could, we think, have been much better done if only they had asked us. No one had asked them. I watched them as they hunched their shoulders and, with a laugh and a wry grin, pulled on and buttoned up their coats more closely, as if to keep their own world safely in. They sank their hands deep into their pockets. Unwanted and thwarted by the world, a little tired of being pushed around; the hidden ache of yet another failure showed in their sad eyes. All they could do was hug their secret sadness to themselves, as bravely they stepped forth into the fresh cold air.

I thought of St. Augustine of Hippo in North Africa, who in his own time had found a problem not unlike our own. His world, the only world he'd ever known, he found in his old age had nearly gone, and he was almost left alone. The sack of Rome, the disintegration of the Roman Empire and of all the values for which he had fought so hard, and then the Pelagian heretics, despite all he could say and do, sweeping all before them, through the places he loved best; he watched it all. If the present was disastrous, the future looked even more foreboding. But for that future which he could not see he knew, though he was old, that he must prepare his own small flock. To comfort his beloved converts and strengthen their faith for the perilous days which so clearly lay ahead, he preached, and wrote vast tomes.

He had to teach them the faith so that they would be faithful, loyal to God's commandments and to his revelation of himself through Christ his Son. He had to train them too. Some had to be so prepared that they would not be content simply to produce a duplicate, in the new world which would perforce emerge, of the old world they had known and loved so well. Some, he found, had no sense of history, and were willing—even eager—to jettison the wisdom of the past. What Christians and pagans had laboriously built up over hundreds of years was, to those who were simply ignorant, of little worth. They did not realize that they had lived out all their lives within a world transformed by the love of God for man; that once that message was lost or was denied, the very fabric of all they loved and took for granted would crumble into thin air, and they would have to live in silent torture, thinking about a lost world which really might have been. And there were many men who sought safety in rejecting all that the new order had to offer; they closed their ranks and talked incessantly about tradition, and wanted to live happily in a past peopled by reason and emotion, not by faith. Bewitched by the haunting dreams of an unreal world, a world not their own, a world indeed which no man had ever known, they sought safety behind closed doors, lest the Stranger might enter in. Indeed they had hoped, but now they hoped no longer.

To such as them, St. Augustine stressed the importance of both permanence and change. 'God, the unchanging Conductor, as well as the unchanged Creator of all things that change' was the God in whose presence they were all called to live their lives. They needed, as he stressed, a lively faith so that their hearts might be attuned to pick up that divine melody which God communicates to all men in so many diverse ways, through words and people, and even through human disasters and quite ordinary things.

As I thought of my good friends now leaving the pub, I wondered how we can attune our ears, and those of others too, so that we may be faithful and hear the word of God as he speaks to us and ever calls us to follow him still further through the maze of life. They lived a life, as they thought, in the world, a real life they might well have said. Yet much of this life of theirs was lived in a dream-world which had never been; they seemed unaware of any need to try to come to terms with this harsh, unheeding world with which each of them in his own way was at odds. How can we tune our ears, and those of others too, so that our troubles and dreams, our worries, hopes, and loves, are all transmuted and become part of that new life which God became man to bring—not to the clever and learned, and those wise in their own conceits, but to simple men like these?

The problem is as old as time, for God gave this new life to men from the beginning of the world; a problem though which now seems far more urgent since Christ has called on us to work with him. Christian missionaries have forever sought an answer. To teach the faith to those who share our language, culture, and scale of basic human values is difficult enough; to teach those who have had a different outlook from their earliest days is a more formidable task. So many of these good men in the pub were fast falling into this more difficult class of men. Further to train them, so that the faith would have vital meaning for them in the lives they had to lead, was a real problem. How could this be done? A good mother, like that poor young mother missing from the pub, has to train her children for the unknown which lies ahead. Each person needs his own charisma if he is to incorporate into his own life that richness which the good God offers him each day. But how are his ears ever to be attuned so that he will hear God speaking to him through bosses who are intolerant of wasted minutes, and through lorries roaring through the night, and through the endless row of nappies on the line, and through the incessant demands of impatient motorists who want more petrol NOW, and through the dull and dreary lectures in the polytechnic, and through those dreary days and nights concerned above all with the filling in of time? How do we, can we, hope to achieve this very simple thing?

The publican behind the bar, who had watched his clients come and go, took off his jacket and rolled up his sleeves. As he locked up the pub he knew his day had just begun. The real work of the publican went on unseen, in the hidden cellars far below, and if that was not well done his beer would be off and his customers would quickly go elsewhere. He had spent his life trying to serve, and he had few illusions left. He'd met too many people, listened in on too many arguments not to know that man, of all the good God's wonderful creations, is the most unreliable, unpredictable, chancy, haphazard, fortuitous of all. Only better beer than could be found elsewhere could ensure their custom, whatever they might say. He must get on to work.

He liked people, and wanted to see them happy. He would have been delighted with the crippled boy who so loved his pint and his friends. With a cheery 'What's yours?' he always tried to chuff up the lonely and depressed. It was the most natural thing in the world for the lorry-driver and the farm labourer and the fair-haired girl in her distress, and all the others too, to regard him as their counsellor, confessor, and friend. In days gone by as he listened to their stories he'd have suggested that the vicar or the parish priest could help. Could they today? He was not so sure. It was the age of the laity. Perhaps it was they who should help his friends adjust their sights.

The clergy, he said, talked of the Church in the world, but in a curious way they were far less in it than they had ever been. They sought to identify with modern man, to work in factories, to look the same as ordinary men, but was their message any clearer? The more they tried to identify, to be what they were not, the more they seemed to be acting out a role which was not theirs, and trying to be what they were not meant to be. What were they meant to be? Not just themselves, or why were they priests at all? The more they tried to be themselves, the more they had to act out a role—even a pious holy role—the less they had to give. He thought, regretfully, that they could not help. Perhaps it was after all the age of the laity, because the clergy had failed. Was that, he wondered, why vocations had dried up so fast? They were, he thought (and he had no facts to get in the way of his own reasonings), being trained all wrong. Trained to serve, to do a job like his, to give what people needed, now a whisky, a martini, a gin, or a simple beer. To serve. But more was needed. They had to teach the truth—he was a Catholic and was quite clear on this—and that, he sometimes thought, they were not trained to do. Their ideas, and their sometimes stereotyped answers from learned books, and their natural selves were not enough. Were they on fire with the love of Christ, was Christ their friend, he wondered sadly—but who was he to speak? (He was well-meaning, but could be an awfully gloomy chap.)

Would you, he wondered, become a publican if you knew that, when you had worked up your public image and built your car park and your clientele, you were then liable to be moved on to another pub and to have to start again? How often could you take such violent interruptions and unwanted changes if you really loved your pub and the friends you'd made? Was the priest's life so very different? Would you advise a younger man to go in for a priest's life, with its built-in frustrations? True, he could accept such difficulties as stepping-stones to God. Was that, he wondered, the best, or only, way of serving God? There are other ways the laity could choose where the structure of the Church had far less say, and where their mission would be less obstructed. But perhaps the zealot needed that frustration, without it the charismatic could so easily go off into an orbit all his own. What was the better part? How should one opt?

How difficult, he thought, to get things right. The saints lived in a world of their own. Was that the answer? He was a fool. Perhaps there was no answer—and just as each man had has favourite drink, so should his life reflect the sort of service he was prepared and meant to give. Perhaps that was what the priest was meant to be. Was that what a 'vocation' really meant? For him to be a publican was a job, but for the priest to be a priest was to be himself, for that was what God had called him to be. He wiped his mouth and poured himself, though it was now long after hours, a long last drink. It was nice to feel he'd sorted things out for God.

Something of that good publican, shut up and working in his closed pub alone, had gone off with his friends. More than a kindly message, a kindly word. It has, I think, been truly said that no man begins to live until he lives in others; so is our faith suspect unless, like salt, it savours all our lives; unless, like an inner light within us, it shines forth on the present world and culture in which we live. If it does less, then do we indeed deny our faith. Somehow this faith I have, this faith which is all-important, must be shared and given, or it will surely die. This means I must talk and enter into dialogue; but to do that will mean that I too will change. The paradox comes back and back all through our lives, and will not go away; to live is to grow, to become what we are not and were not, and yet unless we do that very thing we die; but if we do it, then we find our identity is not lost, but transmuted. Transformed, it grows and flashes with a new fire, like a living gem. A jewel unsuspected lies in the hearts of things and people too, and of disasters and quite ordinary events. It is not as if we are being called to play a role for which in our hearts we know we are unprepared; we are not even asked to do 'a job in the world' as though God could not do it without our help. He only asks us to live our funny, puzzled lives as he calls us through the maze and gives us as our way his only Son—for our life, if it is indeed to blossom, and the jewel in our hearts is to be discovered, must be fashioned on his. In fact he tells us that the two must become one; our life is to be taken up in his, and we are called to share his life for ever. For Christians it must be Christ who is to be the Alpha and Omega of our lives. There is no other way, and this way is enough.

No longer are the difficulties so insuperable when we begin to understand—not only with our heads, but with our hearts, and in our own lives too—that in the love and following of Christ those impossible, yes, impossible, problems, to which we think there can never be an answer, dissolve into thin air. Our hearts can once again rejoice. We may not be, nor ever will be, learned theologians, but we all know something about love. That is perhaps the only thing we know, but that alone is all we need, can we but live it.

But that, of course, we also know, is what we cannot do, nor ever will be able to, without that grace from God. He calls, as always in the Gospel and in the Psalms and the Old Testament too. His call is quite unchanging—'Come' is the word with which he calls the Apostles, and those who seek to know where he lives and is to be found; 'Come to me, all who labour and are heavy laden'; 'Come after me'. No wonder the Psalmist urges us all to 'Come and adore him'. Always a drawing, an invitation, a calling through all time, through all our lives, in countless ways.

There are so many other aspects of his love which affect us all, but perhaps this is the most important, and the one which seems so often to be forgotten when we indulge in moral indignation about the evils in the world. Those evils are real enough, and most of us are all too conscious of the misery and unhappiness and injustice and cruelty and frustration which we can see at every turn. We need, I think, encouragement to look a little deeper, to see things in perspective, to bring that message of faith and hope and love into the world. That message, and that alone, we know can change the hearts of men. If that is done, there is no need to fear. If that is not done, all other efforts will be in vain. No money or diplomacy or power can ever hope to change the hearts of men.

Those good men and women in the pub for whom I tried to write these words by now had journeyed forth into the real world, and only their memory remained. Oh what a fool I'd been. If only I had praised them more as they deserved, that would have helped. A little recognized success would have encouraged them to surmount their own personal problems, and much would have been gained; but not enough. Even alone they could do much more than they were doing—but united in their ideals, fired with a common faith, they could transform the world. An exaggeration? Who would care to dispute what the Holy Spirit could do through half a dozen men and women drinking up their pints, and through the girl at home looking after her poor mites? But they would need to be more than social friends, they would need to be a team, friends in the Lord, trained the only safe way by Christ himself in the Eucharist. Then, and only then, could one be sure that they would be true to all that was best in them, and true to Christ Our Lord who could build upon their faith his own life which alone can both save the world from itself and transform the lives of those who trust in him. What we so often see as an optional extra for the devout is needed by us all. We cannot ask for more, nor for long be satisfied with less. Why then should we indulge our fears any more? If he says: 'Fear not, it is I', we can and should take courage and follow him when he speaks to our hearts and just says 'Come'; enough is said. People, not causes, are at the roots of things.

18 Insights at nightfall

WHEN the sun so splendid sinks beneath the sea,
the clouds like us take on a colour not their own,
they shine for a brief spell with dazzling glory,
then slowly fade; the darkness hiding all.

The air, once warm and friendly,
now, suddenly, turns chill;
the harmony of all things, so visible when the sun is in the sky,
is lost to sight once night is here.

The thin dark line which separates sky and sea
has long since vanished and they have merged together;
as did yesterday merge into today, today into tomorrow;
so our experiences, imaginations, fears, dreams and
        personal decisions
are welded together out of many disparate things.
Only the dull roar and the white fluorescence of the
        breakers

show life continues in that darkening world before the stars
    have risen.
The oneness we experience cannot now be seen, persisting
    in the darkness.
From chance? From providence? From God? From me?

The prattle of the children masks the upsurge of new life
and ever-changing patterns as identities develop and new
    challenges arise.
Apparently alone, granite-like, stolid, containing walls
next to huge boulders, steep cliffs, combining mother and
    child,
man and nature, separately united in resisting
the sea and all erosion which would separate and divide.

The muscles of the heart last longer than the stronger steel,
the child, like a seashell, tossed this way and that,
battered, bruised, purified, refined,
is strengthened, now a living part of a greater whole.

Dee's children cannot grow unless trained to growth
    through giving,
pruned by depression, defined and sharpened to a point
through confrontations, conflicts, tensions, so that they can
    write
their personal choices in their book of life,
giving thanks and praise to the Lord with all creation
for all things,
not by chance, nor by the will of man
but by God's providence leading them on
to the unknown where mystery, wonder and awe for ever
    reign.

They meet false gods, idols of the world today;
security, efficiency, success which they can see,
lengths of cloth cut off the loom,
growth which can be measured, harvests garnered into barns,

tempted to be master of their destiny, lords of everything,
blinded by power, knowledge, slaves to their own conceits,
deafened by the plaudits of senseless adoring mobs ever
    willing to worship
feet of clay; disaster lies that way.

But crushed, coerced, forced to reflect,
to see new visions, insights, Angels' wings
protecting, stimulating them to new friendships and work
    for the Lord,
for the poor, the lonely,
those never represented,
always destined to be dispossessed, who cannot help
    themselves
and zigzag happily, from one enterprise to the next,
through the maze of life,
unwanted, rejected, despised by a stupid world
which puts its faith in bureaucrats, blue-prints, the wit of man,
concrete, technology, the wisdom of the past—now can
    they understand?

The infinite must break into our life if we are to be uplifted
and escape the disaster of success conceived by human
    minds
which would reduce God's plans to ephemeral, transient
    things;
the beauty of the weak, the unexpected, unwilled,
    unwanted Visitor and Stranger
whose coming breaks our fetters and frees us from our
    chains. Praise him.

New unthought-of chapters being written in our book of
    life
as we look on and watch the finger of God's right hand
tracing our story in that dust from whence came forth our
    being
when he breathed into it the life which is his own.

The gift of life God gives us holds together
our past, present and all that is to come,
like a jar in the potter's hand,
as living branches of that body whose life we share with
        him.

His life gives our personal identity a dimension which on
        earth we cannot see,
enriches every moment with a note, a gleam of colour,
forming under the eye of the Conductor a living harmony,
where space, time, matter, mother–child relationship,
        husks of forgiven sin,
frustrations, grief, joy, happiness, laughter,
all we have known, are caught up, digested, charged,
        pruned to form
a living branch of Christ's glorious Vine.
Each lived-through experience, initiative we have planned
has a depth, a resonance, a meaning
for me and for mankind,
which only with the wisdom of hindsight
can we begin to understand.

We flounder like the salmon in the cold cascading water,
out of breath, our vision clouded,
our ears deafened by the roar.

We see the book of life is closing, the final end in sight,
with chapters still unwritten, final messages not yet given,
so much we cannot hope to comprehend.
The unity, the harmony, within, without, is hidden;
we feel lost and quite bewildered; our service not yet
        finished.
Praise him. The work which lasts at least is done.

The book is shut. The shadows over. Eternity begun.
We reap what we have sown;
we are what we have woven,

as we were jostled in the pub;
as we went our separate ways,
as we stumbled, shilly-shallied,
like shuttles rebounding through the warp and weft of life,
now using, now abusing the gifts the good God gave us,
weaving a pattern unutterably our own.

The props, no longer needed, lie discarded.
The book of life, the woven cloth, half finished
with a unity which was hidden,
revealed as part of a living whole;
our lives completed by a life which we were given,
which was never just our own.
The truths we learnt as children upon our mother's knee,
the covenant, the promises God made us,
the peace and joy we glimpsed,
the hopes we hardly dared to entertain,
the hints, the whispers, glimmerings, scarce-felt caressing
    kisses,
the gentle Spirit breathed on us as we lay half asleep,
the light God shone in our hearts
bringing us the knowledge of God's glory
shining in the face of Christ
and in our fellow men.
The pledges, foretastes, buds of a longed-for future,
the mercy of a Father who is our friend,
fulfilled in heaven
when with the living life of Christ
at last we really see
and so grow fully into that somebody who from our
    baptism on earth
we were always meant to be.

All signs and symbols can safely be dismantled
once the storm is over and the lasting Day has dawned.
        Each lonely furrow united with its fellows
        producing seeds of glory

once lay hid beneath the fields of golden grain.
Each bunch of grapes, the wine of life eternal,
symbol of families, friendship, communities, kith
    and kin
united pressed together, preserves for ever
a flavour inalienably its own.
Each colour of the rainbow, quite distinct,
like friends, they melt together
then brilliantly shine forth, banishing the mists of
    darkness,
the new light revealing a truth we'd never seen.
Each child now born on earth, reality and symbol
of God's love, and of the human love of men and
    women too
revealing Christ forever risen
reigning in heaven.

The life we thought we'd woven uncovered as part of the
    cosmic whole,
a filling up of Christ's own work in time.
Each life finding in the words of the Psalmist,
    the fullness of joy in your presence,
    at your right hand happiness for ever
through gladly recognizing what has come to be;
the life of God, of Father, Son, and Spirit
working within what once were mortal frames,
building them up as 'living stones'
so that they live as members of Christ's own body
with one life which now all can see.
    That they may be one
    As Thou, Father, in Me,
    and I in Thee,
    that they may be one in us.
No wonder, on earth, the mystery lies hidden
before the fullness and glory of the whole has been
    revealed.

Notes

page 2   poem by author (hitherto unpublished).

11   Gerard Manley Hopkins, 'God's Grandeur'.
      Ecclesiastes 3:1–8 (Jerusalem Bible).

17   Margaret T. Monro, *A Book of Unlikely Saints* (Longmans, Green, 1943), pp. 131–66.

20   Augustine, *Confessions*, X.xxix.40.

23   Gerard Manley Hopkins, 'God's Grandeur'.

24   Hopkins, 'As Kingfishers catch fire . . .'

33   Viktor E. Frankl, *Man's Search for Meaning* (Hodder & Stoughton, 1964).

47   John 15:5 (JB).

49   Acts 8:32–3 (JB).

53   George Herbert, 'The Flower'.

67   Psalm 15 (16):5–7, Grail/Gelineau version (Collins, Fontana books, 1963).

68   Address by Sir Kenneth Wheare published in the periodical *Oxford*, vol. xxvi no. 1.

81   *A Handbook on Guadalupe* (Franciscan Marytown Press, Kenosha, USA, 1974).

100   2 Peter 1:19–21 (JB).

110   Romans 12:4–5 (JB).

114   Colossians 2:9 (JB).

118   Francis Thompson, 'The Kingdom of God'.

128   Peter Brown, *Augustine of Hippo* (Faber, 1967).

129   Ezekiel 8:3.

130   Brown, op. cit., p. 104 (see also Augustine, *Confessions*, VII.xx.26).
      John Henry Newman, *Apologia Pro Vita Sua*, ed. Svaglic (Oxford University Press, 1967), p. 26.
      The Sermons and Devotional Writings of Gerard Manley Hopkins, ed. Christopher Devlin, S.J. (Oxford University Press, London, 1959), pp. 198–9.

131   1 Thessalonians 2:13 (JB).

132   Colossians 1:12–20 (Revised Standard Version).

140   T. S. Eliot, *Four Quartets*, 'Burnt Norton'.
      Wisdom 8:1 (RSV).

152 John 12:24 (RSV).
153 *Letters of Gerard Manley Hopkins to Robert Bridges*, ed. C. C. Abbott (Oxford University Press, London, 1935), pp. 221, 222.

John 15:5 (JB).
159 John Henry Newman, *Verses on Various Occasions*, 'The Pillar of the Cloud' (Longmans, Green, 1912), p. 114.
163 John 11:25–6 (JB).
Romans 14:8–9 (JB).
John 14:2–3 (JB).
164 Colossians 3:2–4 (JB).
165 1 Corinthians 2:9 (RSV).
Colossians 3:1 (RSV).
166 John 19:26–7 (RSV).
Romans 8:22–3 (JB).
178 Ephesians 1:9–10 (RSV).